58 62

MW01059205

Tom
Peters

*RE*INVENTING WORK:

ALFRED A. KNOPF, INC.

NEW YORK 1999

the

brand you

50

Or: FIFTY WAYS TO TRANSFORM YOURSELF FROM AN "EMPLOYEE" INTO A BRAND THAT SHOUTS DISTINCTION, COMMITMENT, AND PASSION!

This Is a Borzoi Book
Published by Alfred A. Knopf, Inc.
Copyright © 1999 by Excel/A California Partnership

www.randomhouse.com

Grateful acknowledgment is made to Perseus Books Publishers
for permission to reprint excerpts from *Creating You & Co.* by
William Bridges. Copyright © 1997 by William Bridges and
Associates, Inc. Reprinted by permission of Perseus Books
Publishers, a member of Perseus Books, L.L.C.

Library of Congress Cataloging-in-Publication Data
Peters, Thomas J.
    The brand you50: fifty ways to transform yourself from an
"employee" into a brand that shouts distinction, commitment,
and passion! / by Tom Peters. — 1st ed.
        p.   cm. — (Reinventing work)
    ISBN 0-375-40772-3
    1. Career development.   2. Success in business.   I. Title.
II. Series.
    HF5381.P472   1999
650.1—dc21   99-33614
                                                   CIP

Manufactured in the United States of America
First Edition

DEDICATION

MJ, Oprah, and Martha,* inventors of modern Brand You

---

*For the one-in-a-hundred-thousand who doesn't "get it": Jordan, Winfrey, and Stewart. (Real Brand Yous don't need full names!)

The fundamental unit of the new economy is not the corporation but the individual. Tasks aren't assigned and controlled through a stable chain of management but rather are carried out autonomously by independent contractors. These electronically connected freelancers—e-lancers—join together in fluid and temporary networks to produce and sell goods and services. When the job is done, the network dissolves and its members become independent agents again, circulating through the economy, seeking the next assignment.

—Thomas Malone and Robert Laubacher,
"The Dawn of the E-lance Economy,"
Harvard Business Review

50 LISTS: CREDO

CUBICLE SLAVES ... HACK OFF YOUR TIES ... FLIP OFF YOUR HEELS ...

THE WORK CAN BE COOL!

THE WORK CAN BE BEAUTIFUL!

THE WORK CAN BE FUN!

THE WORK CAN MAKE A DIFFERENCE!

Y-O-U CAN MAKE A DIFFERENCE!

BASH YOUR CUBICLE WALLS!

RIP UP YOUR DILBERT CARTOONS!

THE WHITE COLLAR REVOLUTION IS ON!

90 PERCENT OF OUR JOBS ARE IN JEOPARDY!

TAKE CHARGE OF YOUR LIFE!

SUBVERT THE HIERARCHY!

MAKE EVERY PROJECT A WOW!

BE DISTINCT ... OR EXTINCT!

IT'S A NEW MILLENNIUM: IF NOT NOW ... W-H-E-N?

5 0 L I S T S :
S E R I E S   I N T R O D U C T I O N

We aren't knocking Dilbert. Who would dare? But we do believe that work can be cool. THAT THE WORK MATTERS.

—Tom Peters

Work—yours and mine—as we know it today will be reinvented in the next ten years. It's as simple as that. And as profound. Here's why ...

The tough old union militant remembers. In 1970 (not exactly an eon ago) it took 108 guys some five days to unload a ship full of timber. And now? Container daze: eight guys ... one day.

It happened on the farm when the thresher came along. It happened in the distribution center when the forklift arrived. And it happened dockside.

But, hey, it's the new millennium. Ninety-plus percent of us—even in so-called "manufacturing" companies—work at white collar jobs. Fact: We haven't touched—or really even bothered with—white collar productivity. Never. Until now ...

It's a brand-new ballgame. THE WHITE COLLAR REVOLUTION IS ON! The accounting "shop" is coming under the same productivity searchlight that those docks did. And we think we have an inkling of what the new rules will be.

The revolution: Information systems. Information technology. Enterprise Resource Planning systems. Intranets.

Knowledge-capital-management schemes. Enterprise Customer Management. The Web. Globalization. Global deregulation. Etc. Etc. All fueling a—no hype—once every 100, 200, 500(?) years revolution.

Which brings us to this new series of books—which aims at nothing less than a total reinvention of work (how we think about it, undertake it, bring ourselves to it). The work-reinvention revolution turns out to be a matchless opportunity for liberation—in our organizations and in our own lives.

This book is part of the first release in a series of what we call 50lists. Each book describes a different aspect of work in the New Economy. Each book is built on 50 essential ideas.

—The Editors

CONTENTS

1. Coping rests on your shoulders. Forget "they." This is your life. Period. **12**

1a. When was the last time you asked: WHAT DO I WANT TO BE? **17**

2. You have no option: THE WHITE COLLAR REVOLUTION IS ABOUT TO SWALLOW ME/YOU/US! **21**

3. *The* Answer: Becoming "Brand You." **24**

3a. What if we each had "market cap"—free-market evaluation of our economic worth, like ballplayers and actors more or less do? **29**

4. Getting started now: Perform a Personal Brand Equity Evaluation. And: Create a Yellow Pages ad for … you. **32**

4a. We need a snapshot: What does Brand You "look" like? "Feel" like? For starters: Consider Icon Woman. (And hear her roar!) **37**

5. Forget "tasks." The new Brand You currency: WOW Projects! **41**

5a. Commit yourself fully to The Project Life. Pursue Mastery. **43**

6. You—Brand You—are a "package." **46**

7. "Inc." yourself. Mindset: I AM A COMPANY. **49**

8. Speak out! BRAND YOU IS ABOUT WHAT YOU VALUE! **52**

9. No walk in the park: Brand You demands a rich, diverse portfolio of skills. **54**

9a. Brand You Warriors wear at least Eight Hats… from sales to accounting to product development. **57**

10. Learn to play The Great Game of Business. You must master the Brand You Economic Basics. **61**

11. Paint a compelling, technicolor word picture of who you are. **65**

12. OBSESS ON YOUR…JOB TITLE.(Yes, it *is* that important.) **68**

13. Brand You: WALK THE TALK.("We must become the change we want to see in the world." —Gandhi) **71**

14. Brand Yous embrace the real-world Politics of Implementation.(Or else!) **74**

15. Turn crummy little tasks into Hopelessly Cool Projects.(IT CAN—ALWAYS—BE DONE.) **77**

15a. Work with what you've got! Make it a masterpiece! **79**

16. Master "bootstrapping." LEARN TO SCROUNGE RESOURCES! **83**

17. YOU ARE YOUR PORTFOLIO: Think Quality of Project *Portfolio*. **85**

17a. You *are* the WOW-ness of *every* project. So: *Score* WOW-ness! **88**

18. *FOCUS!* **91**

19. You *are* your Clients I: BRAND YOU IS *DEFINED* BY HER (HIS) CLIENTS. Who they are. Who they aren't. **95**

20. You are your Clients II: SO … LISTEN TO 'EM! CONNECT WITH 'EM! **98**

21. You are your saleable competencies: Brand You must be … *stunningly good at something of value to clients.* **101**

22. You *are* your Rolodex I: BRAND YOU IS A TEAM SPORT. **104**

22a. Loyalty: *More* important than ever! New—Brand You—Loyalty = Rolodex Loyalty. (Not "logo loyalty.") **108**

23. You are your Rolodex II: Breadth counts! Collect Freaks! **110**

24. DESIGN MATTERS … A LOT … TO BRAND YOU! You are your "signage": phone skills, report writing style, letterhead, etc. **113**

25. Consider your "product line." *Add* to your product line … regularly. (OR ELSE.) **116**

26. Think B-i-g. As in, Big Ideas. "Did it make me gasp when I first saw it?"—adman David Ogilvy's WOW Test. **119**

27. Me Inc./Brand You Mantra: DARE … DAILY. **121**

28. SUBMIT TO THE PERFORMANCE! Brand You is a performing art. **123**

29. Bosses: YOU GOTTA—damn well oughta—LOVE BRAND YOU! (It's all about turning "employees" into Performance Maniacs.) **127**

30. Identity = Most cherished Asset. Brand You: Learn to think like Gillette or Saturn. **129**

31. A brand is a "trust mark": Brand You rests upon bedrock called *Credibility*. **132**

32. It may sound small. IT AIN'T. Calling Cards tell a Large Tale. (First Things First.) **135**

33. BUILD A WEB SITE THAT WOWS. NOW. **138**

34. You are your own P.R. agency. For starters: Join Toastmasters. **141**

35. Work on your Optimism. (Spreaders of doom + gloom rarely attract followers!) **146**

36. Renewal = Job 1 For Brand You. Period. **149**

37. A must: FORMAL RENEWAL INVESTMENT PLAN. **153**

38. Learn from … anyone. Anywhere. Any time.
BECOME A SPONGE … for Cool Stuff.
(Work on exposing yourself to cool stuff.) **156**

38a. Love the Plateau! Learning—the essence of Brand You—is not a smooth ride. (You get stuck at times.) **163**

39. YOU—Brand You—NEED A TERRIFIC BOARD OF DIRECTORS. (No kidding.) **166**

40. YOU—Brand You—NEED A "FRONT LINE UNIVERSITY." Message: stay in close touch with "real people." **169**

41. Hunt for Cool Dudes-Dudettes. All Brand Yous—youngest to oldest—are perpetually in the Talent Scout Mode. **172**

42. Create your own, cool organization … Me & Co. … even if you are young, "unempowered," and on

someone's payroll. (You are *always* a Builder! If you're smart.) **175**

43. Leadership is me … as Brand You … at all times. ("Leadership" is independent of formal position. *Period.*) **177**

44. POWER MATTERS. Stuff that matters—that gets done—demands superb political skills. **181**

45. YOU—Brand You—NEED A FORMAL MARKETING PLAN. **184**

45a. Think hard: DO I REALLY HAVE A "PRODUCT"? (This is no easy "test" to pass.) **186**

46. Think: ONE WOMAN (MAN) *GLOBAL* POWERHOUSE. (Seriously.) **190**

47. Sell. SELL. *SELL!!!* **192**

48. YOU—Brand You—GOTTA BE A "CLOSER." (Learn to "Ask for the business.") **194**

49. Effective Brand Yous Are dis-loyal! (I.e., on a Crusade that transcends "the corporation.") **196**

50. *WELCOME TO FREE AGENT NATION!* **198**

The Movement 200

Recommended Reading 202

Acknowledgments 204

the brand you

50

INTRODUCTION

In times past, you could be obscure yet secure—now that's harder.
—Michael Goldhaber, *Wired*

Don't compromise yourself, honey. You're all you've got.
—Janis Joplin

About two years ago I realized I was no longer a person but a brand.
—Martha Stewart

1954. College degree. (The lucky ones.) Then off to work for GE. Or GM. Or AT&T. (AT&T's fast-track management program at the Long Lines division nearly snared me in 1964; then Lyndon Johnson started a little war, and I got volunteered.) Don't make waves. Keep your nose clean. Answer the question, "What do you do?" with a proud "J.C. Penney" or "AT&T." (Your company name = Your identity ... as a h-u-m-a-n.) The years pass. Kids off to college. Then they're married. Then grandkids. Age 55. Gone. Age 65. Arrived. Maudlin retirement party. Forty-two years of solid "service." Good corporate citizen. Pensioned off. Away to the time-share condo in St. Pete.

That's the way the post–World War II game was played. Until about 1975. Then came foreign competition. (At first in steel and cars.) (The end of American hegemony.) And the computer finally moved beyond automating accounts receivable.

And then ... **all Hell broke loose.** What do you figure? About 1985? "Foreign competition" became no-shit globalization. "Computerization" moved to the desktop ... and networked systems arrived. And ... welcome, EDI. (Electronic Data Interchange. We won't process your invoice unless it's electronic.—Wal*Mart.) And then ...

The Web.

Layoffs migrated from UAW and UMW and USW Workers to the $100,000-income, 27-year IBM vet next door. (Right before Maggie, his eldest of three, headed off to Middlebury ... with its gajillion-dollar tuition.)

That is, "this stuff" got personal! "Chainsaw" Al Dunlap. And that nice Robert Allen at AT&T ... who laid off more people than Dunlap. And "Dr." Michael Hammer's "re-engineering." (Euphemistically called "right-sizing." No wonder we take such a shine to Dilbert's unvarnished cynicism!)

Dunlap is an ass! "Right-sizing" is an abominable term. But that doesn't turn the clock back. Fact is, the White Collar Revolution is ... finally ... here. And the Genie ain't goin' back into the bottle. In fact, the Genie—ERP/ Enterprise Resource Planning systems, The Web, etc.—is just Bulking Up for the Main Event.

Yes ... The White Collar Revolution is finally on. And yes, I believe that 90+ percent of White Collar Jobs will disappear or be reconfigured beyond recognition. Within 10 to 15 years.

But ... you know what?

I think it's cooler than cool. Slicker than slick. *I* think it is (potentially) liberating beyond measure.

I DON'T WANT TO GO IN THE SAME DOOR TO WORK, MONDAY THROUGH FRIDAY, FOR 41 YEARS, LIKE MY DAD DID. I THINK HIS WORK LIFE STUNK. (SORRY, DAD.)

I am as good as my last-next gig. (Period.) (Just as a housepainter is. And Harrison Ford.) I grow ... or perish. (Professionally.) And I like that. And I think it is quintessentially American. Babbitt might not understand. And Dilbert might label me Goody Two-Shoes or Mr. Rose-Colored Glasses. But Ben Franklin—our first "self-help guru"—would get it. And, God knows, so would Mr. Jefferson of Monticello.

Surprising fact: The new, brain-based economy is really the Old Economy. It asks us—Davy Crockett style—to live by our wits. To improvise. ("We're in a brawl with no rules"—that's the way Xerox CEO Paul Allaire describes our New Economy.)

Your call. Liberating? Or terrifying? Well, if you're sane, the answer—for all of us—is "both." It is scary. All things worth doing are, right? And ... I think ...

Cool-Beyond-Belief.

The answer redux: An Attitude Transplant! I.e.: Begin to think and act like an Independent Contractor. Even if you plan, for the foreseeable future, to stay on someone's payroll. An Independent Contractor is self-reliant. Dependent on her-his skills ... and the constant upgrading thereof. An Independent Contractor has ... in the end ... "only" her-his Track Record. I.e.: her-his Projects.

I call this Independent Contractor-in-Spirit an independent-minded "entity," or perhaps a "brand." More specifically, Brand You. <u>A brand is shorthand. It offer</u>s a <u>promise. Something reliable.</u> ("The pause that re-freshes.") Something phat. ("Just Do It.")

Let's take a quick look. Here's how my colleagues and I contrast a Day-in-Dilbertland-in-"Right-sized"—Towers with the Liberating-New-World-Order-of-brand-new-Brand You:

<u>"BRAND YOU"-WORLD</u>	<u>"EMPLOYEE"-WORLD</u>
Working on a memorable (WOW) project. (If it's not WOW...I'll make it WOW... or bust trying!)	Doing what's assigned.
Committed to my craft. Intend to be incredibly good at s-o-m-e-t-h-i-n-g.	Working assiduously on in-box contents.
Chose this project because it will add to my learning/ because it will s-t-r-e-t-c-h me/because it allows me to hang with cool people.	It's what the boss told me to do. (Give me a break.)
Don't waste a single lunch... networking is my mantra.	Lunch is my business!
I AM A ROLODEX MANIAC.	I hate suck-ups.
Willing to take a "lowly" task if I can turn it into some-thing "cool."	Don't try to push bullshit off on me, bro.
Understand that Projects-Are-Me. *Period.* (This ain't funny: I *am* my project "portfolio.")	I show up. I don't make waves.

"BRAND YOU"-WORLD	"EMPLOYEE"-WORLD
Love the words: WOW … Beauty … Grace … Revolution … Impact.	Give me a f——— break!
L-i-v-e for my Clients!	I do my job.
Purposefully hang out with freaks. (Cool people I can learn cool stuff from.)	My pals are my pals. Lay off.
Think "fun" is cool!	A day at work is a day at work. Don't try to make a congressional case out of it.
Am anxious to get out of bed in the morning.	Another day older and deeper in debt.
Piss some people off. (Because of my strong beliefs.)	Don't rock the boat!
Am (frequently) angry at our slowness to change.	C'est la vie.
Would love to have been with Washington at Valley Forge!	I'm almost vested. Don't tread on me.
Love bright colors!	Gray is beautiful. (Invisibility rules.)
Am action-oriented to a fault.	I AM MEMO MAN!
Embrace life.	There's enough shit that comes your way without asking for more.
Understand that "power" only comes to those who grasp it. ("Pushy" = Good.)	I despise all corporate "politicians."
It's better to ask forgiveness after the fact than permission before. (Always!)	Don't expose your butt.

THE LARGER PICTURE: THE "MODEL"

Our guiding model is simple. And it will be expanded upon in this book and others in this *50List* series. To wit:

The "stuff"—Enterprise Resource Planning Systems, Electronic Data Interchange, company intranets, the Web, etc.—are fueling that once-every-several-hundred-years revolution we referred to in the Series Introduction above.

Point-of-impact for this millennial meteor: the white collar worker.

Those who survive—on or off a corporate payroll—will jettison (almost) everything they've learned and adopt the attributes/attitudes of a PSF/Professional Service Firm. (See our companion book in this series, *the Professional Service Firm50*.) They will behave like independent Brand Yous—the topic of this book. I.e., <u>survivors will "be" a product ... and exhibit clear-cut distinction at ... something</u>.

And the bottom line—the base element—for the PSF, Brand You, and the white collar revolution: <u>the work itself</u>. Or what we call the WOW Project (see *the Project50*).

BRIEF USER'S GUIDE

Building Brand You is a big deal. A personal deal. A high stakes deal. In these pages, we hope we provide a "point of view" as well as a lot of practical suggestions to help you get going.

What follows can be a little overwhelming. The 50+ main items contain within them about 200 "T.T.D.s" ... Things To Do. Any one can soak up a big hunk of time. Hence, we never imagined that you'd try to do everything. Instead we suggest reading as usual, underlining stuff that makes sense. AND ONLY AFTERWARDS PRIORITIZING. For example, you might go back through the book and pick 10 of the 50 "big" items that deserve your urgent attention. (Pick "cool" stuff as well as "important" stuff.) Next, choose one or two "T.T.D.s" from each of the urgent items ... and then get to work.

Caution: As you get practical, which I obviously hope you will, don't lose sight of The Big Picture. In this instance... THE MEANING OF BRAND YOU IN YOUR LIFE.

Brand *You* is as personal as it gets. Brand *You* = Who *You* Are. Perhaps, then, you'll be surprised at how often we say, "Get together with a number of colleagues to consider..." Well, Brand You *is* personal... but it is also a Team Sport. The team, this time, is probably not your formal work group. Instead it's a Collection of Kindred Spirits... Brand You Wannabes, as I often call them in the book. That is, this "stuff" calls for a lot of chewing over. And, we've learned in our training programs, such masticating is immeasurably more effective when a small group of Brand You Seekers gathers together, formally or informally. Hey, for many/most of us this is pretty frightening—if ultimately liberating—stuff. And frightening stuff goes down better with a support group!

You'll use this book your own way, of course, but I hope these suggestions might jump-start the process.

brand you
50

1.

The defining Brand You idea: **"They"** aren't in charge of our careers—and by extension our *lives*—anymore. **We** are. It is up to **us** to fashion **ourselves**.

Young man, make your name worth something.
—Andrew Carnegie

Carpenters bend wood. Fletchers bend arrows. Wise men fashion themselves. —Buddha

Don't just express yourself, invent yourself. And don't restrict yourself to off-the-shelf models.
—Henry Louis Gates, Jr., commencement address at Hamilton College, June 1999

Nobody gives you power. You just take it. —Roseanne

The Nub

It's over! It's over! **Praise God ... it's over.** (That's my view, anyway.) What's over? The world in which "we"—the best and the brightest, the college kids—depended on "them," the Big Corps., to "guide" (micromanage! dictate! control!) "our" careers.

Alas, my Dad was no more than an indentured servant to BG&E...the Baltimore Gas & Electric Co....for 41 years. As I alluded to in the Intro: Same door. West Lexington Street. Day after day. Month after month. Year after year. Decade after decade.

It was no way to live...if living it was.

But..."it" is finished. Kaput. Even if "we" didn't want it to be (and there are literally millions who don't). It is O-V-E-R! New World (Economic) Order: We—white collar "we"—are on our own. Our lives are more precarious. But they've been given back to us. The challenge: What are we going to make of them?

Babbitt is dead. Babbittry is dead. The Organization Man is heaving his Last Gasps.

Enter?

Augie March!

Nobel Laureate Saul Bellow's character begins: "I am an American, Chicago born...and go at things as I have taught myself, free-style, and will make the record in my own way."

It's Emerson II. As in the New/Second Age of Self-Reliance, Ralph Waldo Emerson style.

Ben Franklin (*Poor Richard's Almanack*). Napoleon Hill (*Think and Grow Rich*). Dale Carnegie (*How to Win Friends and Influence People*). Norman Vincent Peale (*The Power of*

Positive Thinking). And: Stephen Covey. Werner Erhard. Tony Robbins. Some sober as pastors. Some raving stage hounds. But the message ... quintessentially American.

America has always been the **Self-Help** Nation. **Bootstrap** Nation. **Pioneer** Nation. In the early years of our democracy, everybody provided for themselves and their families (and their neighbors in time of need). Nobody expected to be taken care of. Self-reliance, independence, and the freedom that goes with them were what we stood for, what defined us. And then, about 150 years ago, when Giant Corp. arrived on the scene (Giant Govt. came about 75 years later), we started to lose "it." Our Franklinian "it." Our Emersonian "it." We succumbed —exactly the right word—to Babbittry. To Big Corp.-That-Will-Be-Mummy-and-Daddy-for-Life.

My take (redux): It stunk **(and stinks)** to high heaven.

But ... Gloria, Gloria, Gloria ... It Is Over!

For a lot of people this is proving to be a very rude awakening, the professional equivalent of learning how to swim by being tossed in the deep end of the pool. This book is about making sure you know you're about to be tossed ... and giving you the tools you'll need not only to survive ... but to thrive/prosper/flourish ... as never before.

Is the prospect frightening?

Hell yes!

Is it a matchless opportunity to lead a fuller, more exciting life? One that forces you to dig a little (a lot) deeper ... but rewards you with growth, pride, and independence (oh yes, and perhaps a lot more money)?

Hell yes!

Can *you* do it?

Yes, you can. (I think ... or I wouldn't have written this book.)

T.T.D. (Things To Do) / This Is Your Life!

1. AA is powerful. It has saved hundreds of thousands of lives ... and souls. Form your own mini-AA. Or ISA ... Indentured Servants Anonymous. Or ... CSA ... Cubicle Slaves Anonymous.

Message: Support groups do help. A lot! They provide an opportunity to get together with folks who are in the same boat as you. This creates an immediate bond ... and the perfect environment to let down your hair ... and discuss with absolute honesty ... your fears (we all have them) ... and hopes (we all need them) ... and plans (we all better have them).

Get together with colleagues—work and nonwork—and talk through this New World (of Work) Order. Terrified? Share it. Read Franklin. And Emerson. And Covey. Discuss them. Think and talk about Y-O-U (selfishness is not only a virtue, it's a necessity … and it'll help the next guy/gal get a handle on his/her dilemma/opportunity). Begin to think of yourself as an Independent Soul. On the make. (In the best sense.)

2. Consider Augie March's world: *"I have taught my-self, free-style, and will make the record in my own way."* What does that mean to you? *Precisely?*

How do you—probably still on a Big Company payroll—take your *f-i-r-s-t* steps toward Psychological Indepen-dence? Write your own Augie March style **D**eclaration of **P**ersonal **I**ndependence.

3. Banish negative thoughts. (What nonsense!) But seriously, paint a Technicolor Picture of how all this "new stuff" could be Cool … for You. I.e.: Liberating. Formally list the current and potential positives…about a New In-dependent You.

4. *Addendum for Bosses:* The best thing you can do for the 18 professionals who "report" to you is to initiate a dialogue about "perceived independence." Hey, as boss I want…desperately…to have folks working for/with me who possess the Free Agent Mentality. I—like the Antarctic Explorers of old—want only volunteers. In this case…**Volunteers for Mission Century Twenty-one.**

1a.

The Nub

I read a single, simple sentence recently.

I remember the jolt:

"When was the last time you asked, 'What do I want to be?'"

The author: Sara Ann Friedman. The book: *Work Matters: Women Talk About Their Jobs and Their Lives.*

Surely you've heard the old joke:

Why do parents keep asking their kids, "What do you want to be when you grow up?"

The parents are hunting for ideas!

WHAT DO YOU WANT TO BE?

My life has turned out rather well, most would say. Certainly I've attained "success" as publicly defined (whatever that is) beyond my wildest dreams.

But still, "it" knocked me for a loop: WHAT DO I WANT TO BE?

"Brand You" is a pragmatic, commercial idea. It's about how to survive as the shit-hits-the-white-collar fan. But it's also about opportunity. And liberation. And definition. (Self-definition.)

I.e.: What do **I** want to be?

What do **I** want to stand for?

Does **my** work matter?

Am **I** making a difference?

None of us, I daresay, ask these questions enough. Not Bill Clinton. Or Al Gore. Or George W. Bush. Or Dan Quayle. (Though maybe Oprah, Martha Stewart, and the Dalai Lama do.)

WHAT DO I WANT TO BE?

My/our message:

FEEL FREE TO ASK YOURSELF "THAT QUESTION"! REGULARLY! (OKAY?)

WORDS

The secret to life is to have a task ... something you bring everything to.... And the most important thing is —it must be something you cannot possibly do.

—Henry Moore, sculptor

Work is my obsession but it is also my devotion.... Absorbedness is the paradise of work.

—Donald Hall, poet and essayist, *Life Work*

[The idea of quitting] was really about the absolute roteness of it all. [Then my boss] gave me a project where I was the only employee. I was able to call myself king, emperor, any title you wanted. And I hired one technician. And from that we built a [multi-billion-dollar] plastics business.

—Jack Welch, CEO, GE, on nearly quitting after his first year with the company (*Fortune*, January 1999)

Her garden is work because it is a devotion undertaken with passion and conviction, because it absorbs her; because it is a task or unrelenting quest which cannot be satisfied.

—Donald Hall, *Life Work*, on his late wife, the poet Jane Kenyon

I think it helps to mind.

—A. E. Housman, Oxford classicist, per Tom Stoppard in *The Invention of Love*

T.T.D./ What Do **I** Want to Be?

1. Take a couple of good pals out to lunch. Or better yet, dinner. Discussion topic: What do I want to be? (I realize that this is advanced clinical psychology. And a big ball of wax. But you do have to start ... somehow ... somewhere.) Idea: Turn bitching-over-the-water-cooler-about-the-consultants-from-Andersen-Consulting-trying-to-define-our-jobs-away into *Hey-What-*

an-Opportunity-to-Redefine-the-Bullshit-Out-of-Our-Jobs ... if-we-can-get-our-heads-screwed-on-Right.

2. What would "Cool Work" look like? Alone ... or better yet (again) with a few pals ... concoct a list of 25 (no fewer!) phrases that define for you/you all ... Work that Matters. Can you somehow apply five of these phrases to your current project? *In the next week?*

3. Try shameless sloganeering (football and basketball coaches do it all the time!). Put up posters: THE WORK MAKES A DIFFERENCE! I AM MASTER OF MY OWN UNIVERSE! WE MATTER! DO NOT DISTURB: DOIN' COOL SHIT! (Or some such.)

4. Think about the ballplayers, hairstylists, carpenters, chefs, and movie stars you admire. How can your work be more like their work? Be very specific. Discuss this with those Long-Suffering Pals I keep talking about. Form a Support Group. Whatever.

DO SOMETHING! GET ON WITH "IT."

2.

The productivity bazooka—after a hundred-year obsession with blue collar work—is aimed at the white collar world. And when the smoke clears ... who will be left standing? Y-O-U!

If (BIG "if") you grasp what's happening ... and respond accordingly.

The Nub

The attention economy is a star system.... If there is nothing very special about your work, no matter how hard you apply yourself you won't get noticed, and that increasingly means you won't get paid much either.

—Michael Goldhaber, *Wired*

This book could readily have been titled *No Other Option.* That is: **Brand You ... or Canned You.**

Is that alarmist talk? Extremist rants? "Yes" on both scores. And ... decisively ... "No."

That is: Your job probably won't evaporate between now and the time you finish reading this book. (At least if you're a fast reader.) But it is going to ... evaporate ... or at the very least be redefined beyond recognition … in the next ten years.

I'm known, I suppose, as a bit of a radical. Well, nothing could be farther from the truth. Look back at *In Search of Excellence*. Called a "revolutionary book" by some. Only 17 years old. And yet … and yet … you won't find "globalization" or "information technology" in the index. Radical!? Radical, Hell! Almost all of my grossest errors in the last 20 years have been errors of … conservatism. Of underestimating the speed and magnitude of change.

So, I repeat … 90+ percent of White Collar Jobs will be totally reinvented/reconceived in the next decade, give or take a year or two.

Thus: Those of us—starting with me!—who want to survive The Flood will grasp the gauntlet of personal reinvention … before we become obsolete. In other words: **"Do unto yourself before the bastards do it unto you."**

T.T.D./Inescapable White Collar Revolution

1. **DO YOU REALLY BELIEVE IN THE COMING APOCALYPSE, SISTERS AND BROTHERS?**
Seriously: Talk about the White Collar Revolution. Study it. Read up on it. (Start—ASAP—a reading group.) Invite gurus in for a Brown Bag Lunch. The Big Idea: ANTICIPATION BEATS REACTION. I.e.: Wouldn't it be cool to be ahead—a little, if possible—of the power curve/tidal wave on this?

2. Set up lunch or dinner dates with four or five people you know who are successful independent contractors. Or invite them in to talk to a small group of your colleagues. Start making a list—a manual of sorts?—of Work Characteristics in the New Economy. (Or something to that effect.) I.e.: Become a student! Do your homework! Study with masters!

3. Aim high! "Be optimistic," is, of course, the ultimate in mindless advice. But do try to paint some **Cool Pictures of What a Cool White Collar World Might Look Like.**

* * *

IT IS THE NEW MILLENNIUM. **YOU CANNOT STAND ON A PAT HAND.** PERIOD. **I can't, either.** I am madly experimenting with different sorts of communications devices … i.e., this series of books; and different media (teleconferencing, the Web, desktop-based training products). Why?

I—AGE 56—GOTTA.

Unless I want to fold my tent and go gently into that freezing night. AND I DON'T! And P.S.: I'm one of the lucky ones with the option (a.k.a. the wherewithal) to call it quits. Unless you've got a trust fund up your sleeve, this radical reinvention of yourself…into Brand You…is a necessity! Unless you fancy yourself retiring to a nice, cozy refrigerator box! (And that, colleagues, is only a small exaggeration. Oh, all right, a not-so-small one. But my point is: **THIS IS YOUR LIFE WE'RE TALKING ABOUT!)**

3.

Translation: **Welcome to the Age** ... *if you're smart* ... **of Brand You.**

The Nub

The yogurt is hitting the fan. With a roaring kerplunk. And few (none?) will escape unscathed. The White Collar Revolution gathers way. Fast. Job security—as we've known it—vanishes.

So ... **what now?**

My answer: **Return to Job Security!** (Not the answer you expected, I bet.) But it's **New** Job Security. Or, actually, Very Old New Job Security. It's what job security was all about before—long before!—Big Corp. Before Social Security. And unemployment insurance. Before there was a big so-called safety net that had the unintended consequence of sucking the initiative, drive, and moxie out of millions of white collar workers.

I'm talking about job security in the Colonies and in the first century after our country was founded. Which was:

* <u>Craft</u>

* <u>Distinction</u>

* <u>Networking skills</u>

<u>Craft = Marketable Skill. Distinction = Memorable.</u>
<u>Networking Skills = Word of Mouth Collegial Support.</u>

It's as old as the colonial blacksmith. (And his modern counterpart, the housepainter. Or local CPA.) As new as Hollywood. Or the peripatetic Web programmers in their apartments in San Francisco or Austin or Raleigh-Durham … or Tahiti.

<u>It's about being so damn good and meticulous and re-</u><u>sponsible about what you do (and making sure that what</u> <u>you do is work that needs to be done) that the world taps</u> <u>a T1-speed path to your PC.</u>

My modern-language (a.k.a. Peters-Speak) term for this ancient, self-reliant, networked, word-of-mouth-dependent, distinguished craftsperson: Brand You.

I'm a believer in Branding. Guided, as I often am, by adman David Ogilvy, I don't think brands are marketing flimflam. The consumer is not an idiot. You can't, by and large, brand crap. And—per Ogilvy—you're a damn fool if you don't brand good stuff: iMACs or Ziplocs or a cool setting for drinking coffee, called Starbucks.

A brand is a "trust mark." It's shorthand. It's a sorting device.

"THE WORD" ACCORDING TO SCOTT

Scott Bedbury helped brand Nike and Starbucks. (Not bad.) I like his description of a brand:

> *A great brand taps into emotions.... Emotions drive most, if not all, of our decisions. A brand reaches out with [a] powerful connecting experience. It's an emotional connecting point that transcends the product....*
>
> *A great brand is a story that's never completely told. A brand is a metaphorical story that's evolving all the time.... Stories create the emotional context people need to locate themselves in a larger experience.*

I don't know about you, but I don't feel in the least bit offended, demeaned, or dehumanized by the thought of Brand You or Brand Me. Or Me Inc., another of my favorites. To the contrary, I think Brand You/Brand Me/Me Inc. ties me rather directly to the Pilgrim Fathers, Ben Franklin, and Steve Jobs—which is a lineage that I far prefer to Organization Man ... let alone Cubicle Slave!

* * *

My friend the artist Annette Lemieux produced a wonderful piece, *I AM* (see reproduction on facing page). Hanging on my wall next to her sophisticated work is a stark, white-on-black full-page ad torn from a popular magazine. It's a Discover Brokerage ad: *YOU ARE THE CEO OF YOUR LIFE.*

1. Got a friend—real estate agent, lawyer, etc.—who's got a real rep in the city, whose name people immediately associate with quality, results, perseverance? (If you don't know any local stars personally, ask around until you find one.) Ask her to spend an evening with you and perhaps a few colleagues, chatting about how she Broke Out of the Pack. Does she have any trademarks—diligent sending of thank-you notes, a certain color scarf, speedy service—that help to define her? That is: Start to infuse those "brand ideas" into your vocabulary/life.

2. Start playing with words. Keep a notebook, paper or electronic. Ask yourself: WHO AM I? WHO AM I **NOT?** (The experts agree: Brand is as much about what a product "is not" as about what it "is.")

3. Start asking yourself every day:

IS WHAT I'M DOING **RIGHT NOW** CONSISTENT WITH BUILDING A BRAND, MY BRAND?

If not, well, wonder about how you're spending your time.

4. Brands aren't built in a day! Walk—don't run!—into all this. Play with the ideas. Define your strengths (and weaknesses). Consider "trademarks." Try the fit. Refine the fit. Be purposeful but not panicky:

THIS IS THE "ESSENCE-OF-YOU" WE ARE TALKING ABOUT. (À la Meryl Streep or Ted Koppel.)

3a.

THAT IS, A MEASURABLE MARKET CAPITALIZATION, THE SAME WAY—IN EFFECT—BALLPLAYERS DO?

The Nub

Business news headlines, circa spring-summer 1999:

MBA: Managed By Agent
> —*Newsweek* on execs' increasing use of agents to manage their careers

Serving Chef Under Glass: Kitchen Celebrities Are Relying on Image Builders
> —*The New York Times* on "the chef as brand"

Agent [Leland Hardy's] goal is to bundle athletes such as Saints first-round draft pick Ricky Williams into "entertainment vehicles."
> —*Chicago Tribune.* Hardy "sees Williams as celebrity, as programming, as vehicle for an amalgamation of 21st Century media markets stretching far beyond the limited imagination of a football field."

DR. KOOP'S BIG COUP

 —Business Week. "What's in a name? If you're C. Everett Koop, try $44.3 million. The former Surgeon General's health-care Net service, Drkoop.com, went public on June 8."

What Am I Bid for These Geeks?

 —from a Wired News Report. On April 27, 1999, eBay, the online auction house, got into the people business. A 16-person Internet Service Provider offered its services to the highest bidder, with an opening bid of $3.14 million required. For that you'd obtain the services of one director, three managers, seven senior engineers, and five administrators.

 Management gurus, if they're wise, have management gurus. One of mine is Stan Davis. (I once, in a syndicated column, called his *Future Perfect* the "management book of the decade." Stan is off on a new wicket, the ultimate information-age wicket. In this odd, emergent "knowledge economy," he declares, we might well all have measured market capitalization. Pro ballplayers and actors and actresses and the Three Tenors already do. David Bowie, in 1997, offered Bowie Bonds. We, the public, could take a ride on his future marketability. This was no PR trick: Prudential bought up the entire $55-million offering. (James Brown became No. 2, to the tune of $30 million in Brown Bonds, in June 1999.)

 Does it sound Seriously Far Out? At first blush, yes. But on second thought...

1. **WHAT IF** … this weren't pie in the sky? I, for one, am not at all sure that it is. It's sorta humorous—if you are a 28-year-old "staff" accountant.

But maybe, **JUST MAYBE,** we ought to think twice. And then twice more. (I am.)

4.

ONE: **Make a PERSONAL BRAND EQUITY
EVALUATION.**

Here's a sample set of elements:

1. *I am known for [2–4 things]. By this time next year,
I plan also to be known for [1–2 more things].*

2. *My current project is challenging me in the following
[1–3 ways].*

3. *New stuff I've learned in the last 90 days includes
[1–3 things].*

4. *Important new additions to my Rolodex in the last
90 days include [2–4 names].*

5. *My public—local/regional/national/global—"visi-
bility program" consists of [1–2 things].*

6. *My principal "résumé enhancement activity" for the
next 90 days is [1 item].*

7. *My résumé/CV is discernibly different from last
year's on this date in the following [1–2 ways].*

TWO: **Develop a ONE-EIGHTH (OR ONE-QUARTER) PAGE YELLOW PAGES AD FOR BRAND YOU/ME & CO.** Some firms—as part of their intellectual-capital development programs—have created formal Yellow Pages documents. If your company were among them, how would your entry read? Would it be WOW!? (Or … not?) This is no casual exercise! Imagine people are shopping for your service. They pick up the Yellow Pages. What can YOU offer them … summarized succinctly and with flair … that *no one else is offering*?

THREE: **Create an EIGHT-WORD PERSONAL POSITIONING STATEMENT.** Now. ("If you can't describe your position in eight words or less, you don't have a position."—Jay Levinson and Seth Godin, *Get What You Deserve!*) Doing this is no walk in the park!

FOUR: **How about a BUMPER STICKER that describes your essence?** A reporter asked a politician running for office in November 1998 to "Describe yourself in a bumper sticker." Nice! How about you? (Redux: No walk in the park.)

The Nub

I'm leaping ahead here. And you'll probably want to read this … forget about it … and then come back to it as you move through the rest of the book. But I think it's important to lay out the bare-bones parameters of the Brand You idea at this point.

The exercise: We live in a very busy, crowded world. You've got to cut to the chase.

What am I? What do I stand for? How do I stand out?

I dislike the whole idea of corporate career counselors. I just don't want Big Brother mucking about with my life. It **is** my life, not theirs!

Sure, I can use professional help (I go to a shrink), but the whole-bloody-point: **I AM CEO OF MY LIFE.** (Big Co. is not going to cosset me—or YOU—no more. Period. And: **Y-E-S!!**)

The point of this book/series:

(1) TAKE YOUR/MY LIFE BACK FROM "THEM." (2) <u>SCREW DILBERT: CYNICISM IS FOR WHINERS. (3) SELF-RELIANCE IS ALL-AMERICAN.</u> (As is, paradoxically, Community-of-Peers Dependence. See below.)

So try some version or subset of the four exercises above. By coincidence, I ran into a very successful personal-care products distributor the night before I wrote this. She said she'd been to one of my seminars in 1998 and had loved the Yellow Pages idea. In fact, she and her partner had made it the centerpiece of their hiring and formal employee-evaluation process. "I used to hate evaluation time," her partner told me. "Now it's actually fun. We work over the Yellow Pages ads together with the associate, and it makes it, to be hackneyed, a 'win-win' conversation between equals." He added that they also insist that every new job candidate create, as part of his or her application portfolio, a Yellow Pages ad. Love it. (More important: So do they.)

* * *

The essence of a Yellow Pages ad:

TOM PETERS, PROVOCATEUR FOR HIRE

Tom's Tantrums: He rants. He raves. He spits statistic after hard statistic … story after story. Then he demands radical action. Tom Peters is on a Mission. To Reinvent Work. To make Each Day Count. For each of us in White Collar World. To crush Dilbertian cynicism. *Business Week* calls him "business's best friend and worst enemy." *The Economist* tags him the über-guru of management. In any case, he's out to shake things up. To rattle every cage. Tom will, says Stephen Covey, rearrange your molecules. Visit with him at www.tompeters.com. Contact him at **tom@tompeters.com.**

JULIE ANIXTER

Value I add in 30 seconds or less …

Making design a visible advantage in business and education. I'm a designer who can take a big idea faster than you can say BIG IDEA and see how to translate it in 15 different cool ways into action, new programming, and products. I believe in education as marketing and marketing as education. I also have a rather eclectic Renaissance Woman's perspective—including an innate love of art and politics, my legacy from my grandfather who was a political boss in Chicago in the twenties. And I'm willing to share it.

ERIK HANSEN

Funny, irreverent, cynical, optimistic, thrill-seeking Gemini thrives on working hard with smart people. Former North Sea fisherman, steel sculptor, glass blower, explosives man, world traveler has settled down . . . to become an anal-compulsive-detail-oriented project manager/editor. Won't work with whiners. Wonders why no one seems to know how to load a dishwasher properly . . .

Guiding motto: from Henry James: Be one on whom nothing is lost.

Motto #2: Work hard. Play hard. Eat well. Buy Art.

Motto #3: If you're not having fun, you're not doing the right thing.

T.T.D./ Brand You Evaluation "Tools"

1. Individual: Start the Process—however haltingly—now. Pick one or two of the tools above. Do a draft Personal Brand Equity Evaluation or Yellow Pages Ad. (Play—right word!—with the other two. It is great discipline.) The idea: Practice talking about your distinction. To start . . . hey . . . YOU'VE GOT TO START!

2. Repeat the above with a (small) handful of pals or colleagues. (The **"Brand You Club"?**)

3. Professional Service Firm "boss":

   * Use one or more of these tools as the basis for an ongoing dialogue with each employee. And

with all employees. (What do we—collectively—stand for? How do we—collectively—stand out?)

* Use these tools as the basis for Formal Evaluation. (And also consider introducing them, per the personal-care products distributor above, in the hiring process!)

4. I don't mean to be testy. (Well, actually, I do.) But if you don't accept the suggestions above ... Why Not? (Got a better idea? Great! Go for it! Just don't stand still.)

4a.

The Nub

Humans "think" visually. A picture really is worth a million words. And great brands have readily identifiable icons—just ask Nike or Apple or Shell—strong, simple images that connect with consumers.

So ... what does Brand You look like?

Wait ... I'm getting ahead of myself here. Before you can create your icon, you need to know what you're trying to communicate with it.

My colleagues and I have wrestled mightily with this. It's taken us months. We decided we would develop an icon for an ideal Brand You—"our" prototypical professional star of early century twenty-one.

We started by asking "who" our Brand You was. We determined that Icon Woman (Man):

* She (he) is totally turned on by her (his) work.

* The work is a WOW Project.

* "It" **M**atters.

* "It" is **C**ool.

* "It" is **B**eautiful. It literally takes your breath away.

* She and her work are "in your face." It makes the establishment cringe, at least a little bit.

* She is an **A**dventurer, a bit of a Pirate.

* She is her own woman, CEO of Her Own Life (even if that life is still on someone's payroll at this moment).

* She's at least a little funky.

* Her tastes are eclectic, her curiosity insatiable.

* She laughs a lot.

* She thinks screw-ups are as normal as breathing.

* She is driven ... and totally committed to her Craft.

* She hangs out with some seriously rad dudes.

* She'll pass up a "prestigious" job in favor of an offbeat project where she can learn something new-different. (I.e.: She sleeps, eats, and breathes renewal.)

* She is not God. She is not Bionic Woman.

She (he) **is** determined to Make a Damn Difference!

Below you'll see our First Draft Icon Person, courtesy of our partner Ed Koren.

Why fret about this?

"They" say an author needs someone to write to. (Writing is very personal, I'll surely grant you that.) So we've tried:

* We want (desperately) an anti-Dilbert character. (I love Dilbert. He's right. He's funny. But I hate the cynicism, except as a wake-up call. It's my life, and I'll not spend it pushing paper in some crummy cubicle. And you?)

* We want a Cool Dude/Dudette, but someone who's not so far out that her persona feels unattainable. (I'm not panicked about having overreached: I think all of us have a fair hunk of spunk in us, spunk that has been systematically repressed by an educational system that basically teaches us what we *can't* do and by hierarchical employers who don't believe we're capable of initiative and invention. Such initiative waits—anxiously! eagerly!—to be released.)

T.T.D./Icon-Person

1. Help us (and yourself)! (PLEASE!) This is practical. (An image is worth thousands upon thousands of words, etc. Hey: True!) Help us/me! Paint pictures of... Liberated You! Liberated Me! Brand You! Brand Me! Me Inc. **What do "we" look ... feel ... smell ... sound ... touch ... taste like?** Please work at this. It is important. And practical. (And if you wish, as I hope you do, we'll discuss it at **www.tompeters.com.** Send ideas/sketches/comments there.)

2. **We are defining New Me/New Us here.** So: Paint word pictures. Real pictures. Think about it. Work with colleagues. It's not a frivolous exercise. NOW: COMPARE YOUR WORD/VISUAL PICTURES WITH *E-X-A-C-T-L-Y* WHAT YOU ARE UP TO AT WORK. AT THIS MOMENT. Discrepancy? How do you start the change process to reduce/eliminate that discrepancy? (I.e.: What *one different thing* can you do today to bring your work-life self into sync with your real, spirited self? E.g.: Hold the weekly staff meeting at the nearby park?!)

5.

"Job"/"tasks" intimate limits and constraints. (E.g., "It's not my job"; "I've got to get this task out of the way by Tuesday.") They connote doing what you're told rather than reinventing the assignment until it sings!

Brand You is about breaking bonds and creating unmistakable value-added "products" (*projects!*) for identifiable "customers." The products/projects become "braggables." The customers become Clients/ Co-conspirators-for-Cool/Raving Fans/Word-of-Mouth-Cheerleading-References.

The Nub

I **AM** MY PROJECTS.

I AM A "PROFESSIONAL SERVICES PERSON." (Have been since 1966.) I am a good Dad or a bad Dad. Not sure which. (Who is?) But professionally ... I am clear:

I **AM** MY PROJECTS.

PERIOD.

I hate—dating back to my Navy days, 30+ years ago —"job descriptions." I've got my own job description.

Did 33 years ago in Vietnam as a 23-year-old Navy Seabee (construction battalion) officer. Do now:

DO COOL SHIT.
EVERY DAMN DAY.
OR DIE TRYING.

I'm not a very religious person. But I do want to count, to matter, to make a difference. The coin—the only coin —of my realm is projects.

Stuff. Stuff with beginnings. Stuff with endings. Stuff with Clients. Stuff with a (personal) Brand Signature.

Stuff that M-a-t-t-e-r-s. Stuff that makes the world a slightly better place. Sound corny? Sorry. Cynicism is for losers. It's easy. It's glib. And it's boring as death itself. Have the courage to be corny! (I have NEVER met a truly successful person who was a raging cynic. Maybe about some things ... but NEVER ... EVER ... about his/her passion/projects! Do you think M. Jordan is cynical about basketball ... M. McGwire about baseball ... S. Spielberg about movies ... P. Lynch about mutual funds ... Oprah W. about television? **NO WAY!** They are true believers all!)

I own my world. People ("they" ... damn "they"!) beat me up. But it is *my world* ... to make ... or mess up. I take full responsibility for my screw-ups. They are not—ever —"the boss' fault."

Life is fickle. Life is rude. Life is unfair.

But it is my life. My projects. P-e-r-i-o-d. (Right?)

And yours, too? **(Eh?)**

T.T.D./ Projects Are Me!

1. Yes? Or: No? P-R-O-J-E-C-T-S A-R-E M-E. Please … think about it. (Hard.)

2. So will "the project" you are working on … right now … make a difference? Will it count? E.g.: Will it make the world a better place (for, say, your customers)?

3. Initiate a dialogue with your colleagues around this: I AM MY PROJECTS. Do "we"—all—buy the act/concept? If so, is *every one* of our projects … Something That Might Count? **(Seriously?!)**

5a.

**COMMIT YOURSELF
WHOLEHEARTEDLY
TO . . . THE PROJECT LIFE.**

The Nub

Journalist George Leonard wrote a marvelous book with a marvelous title: *Mastery*. It is about being consumed by the pursuit of … well … **m-a-s-t-e-r-y** of a skill. Sailing. Or judo. Or cooking. (Or recruiting Cool Talent.)

We expect that level of mastery. Of a **neuro-surgeon**. Of a **cellist**. Or **soprano**. Or **novelist**. Or **NBA power forward.** And, actually, of that **marvelous cabinetmaker** who turns your kitchen into a work of art. (Paul Roberts turned mine into one.)

So why not the "IS specialist"? "Trainer"? "Purchasing Officer"? We rarely use the term … Mastery … in such a setting.

Why not?

Why has Dilbert won? And Mastery lost? I want to reintroduce Mastery. With a vengeance. Mastery and The Project Life.

T.T.D./Mastery and The Project Life

1. Brand You and M-a-s-t-e-r-y. No option. What … *exactly* … does Mastery mean? Ask a surgeon friend. An architect. An artist of some repute. A cabinetmaker with a two-year local backlog.

2. Define … Mastery and The Project Life. What are the attributes thereof? **(List 15.)** Is "it" indeed worth the candle? Worth the sacrifice? (Ask that surgeon … again.) Is your "profession" a true Calling? If not, what, if anything, can you do about it? What are the options, other than changing careers? How could the Projects you undertake be transformed into **S**omething **W**orth **P**ursuing? Specifically? Start with your current project. Talk with your teammates: How could we make this project into a Step Toward Mastery?

3. This is tough. This is personal. This is about who you are. Who you want to be. Take it personally! Start. But don't rush ... don't be too hard on yourself. Proceed with care. Right word: This is all about **c-a-r-e**.

6.

Most of us—save Martha Stewart and a handful of others—don't think of ourselves as "a package." Mistake! Everybody *is* a package. ("He's a ball of fire." "She's a pistol." "He's the biggest bore I've ever met.") The trick for Brand You is making sure you control your package and the message it sends.

Step No. 1: Go to the *grocery*. (No kidding.) Look at packages that grab—literally—your attention. And those that don't. The ones that do (I bet) have: *Energy! Vitality! Clarity! Economy! Surprise! Trustworthiness! Beauty and scintillating design!* Not a bad set of traits for thee or me/Brand You, eh?

The Nub

Packaging [is] the temptation.... It is a tool for simplifying and speeding decisions.... They [McDonald's et al.] are not like a package. They are packages.
—Thomas Hine, *The Total Package*

I can hear what you're muttering: **"Flashy? Me? That's not me! What am I supposed to do? See a surgeon? Get a personality transplant?"**

No!

Fact is … excuse the statement of the obvious … you have a personality. (Ask your close friends!) One of the (big Brand You wannabe) problems: **Many/most of us suppress our personalities between nine and five.** We're afraid to show just how quirky we really are. So we snuff out our spontaneity and eccentricities … and nurture Dilbert-esque resentments toward the boss and/or our co-workers … that manifest themselves as passive aggression. Like doing a half-ass job. Guess who gets hurt the most? (*Hint*: It ain't the boss.)

One of Southwest Airlines' secrets. Yes, they are in a life-or-death business. (They get it: best safety record in the industry.) But they exude p-e-r-s-o-n-a-l-i-t-y because they … ask for it! They ask employees: **P-L-E-A-S-E … don't park your personality in Lot D.** Bring it to work! Express it! Add zest to your peers' and your customers' lives!

Which brings me back to Packaging. Because Packaging is Expressed Personality. For Ford. And Fidelity. For Harvard. And Brown. And McDonald's. And for me. And … for you.

Suppose you did get the ax. And started to sell your services. Either as an Independent Contractor or via a Headhunter.

WHO ARE YOU, ANYWAY? What words and phrases come to mind? Skills? Personal traits? What's distinct?

What separates you from the mass [of trainers, IS specialists]? Why should I—prospective employer—invest $70,000 a year in you? Or $800 per day in your fees for executing a particular project? I.e.: WHAT'S THE "PACKAGE"?

T.T.D./Packaging Brand You

1. Read Thomas Hines's *The Total Package*. And Dale Carnegie's old faithful, *How to Win Friends and Influence People*. Talk to a packaging designer. Visit two or three successful solo practitioners: graphic artists ... lawyers ... accountants. How—specifically!—do they PACKAGE themselves? Do they think about it? If so ... in what terms? Specifically?

2. Start doodling. Pictures. Words. Even songs. WHO AM I? What's my distinction? Why am I a good/great/cool person to have on board an Important Project Team? *Play with this.* (But get started.) Do it alone. With a pal.

3. Do make that trip to the grocery store. Spend an hour. Walk the Mall. Spend two hours. Examine movie ads. Become an aficionado of...**Packaging.** I.e.: Study packaging! Examine packaging! What—exactly—turns you on? Off? And: How do those lessons apply—precisely—to the "selling" of you/Brand You?

7.

William Bridges calls it You & Co. (His provocative book: *Creating You & Co.*) *Fast Company* magazine calls it Free Agent Nation and Unit-of-One. It all begins by your sitting at your desk and saying to yourself: "Okay, I'm still officially at Widgets & Co. But in fact I'm Ms. Free Agent ... on loan to Widgets, Inc. for as long as **I** choose."

The Nub

I AM A COMPANY!

That's the ticket! As of when? **NOW.** At least ... in my head.

The biggest hurdle to Brand You-ness is between your ears. It's learning to Think Independent. And it truly has nothing whatsoever to do with whether you plan to stay with your current company for another six months ... or another 16 years. (Well, it sorta does; if you are even thinking "16 years," you are not serious about The Project Life/Brand You.)

It has everything to do with who you see in the mirror: Company Woman? Or Marge Jacobsen, Independent Actor, vigorously pursuing a path to Distinction and Mastery ... who just happens to work in Finance at USAA ... for now?

Company. **Inc.** Distinct entity. Stands for something. Provides a discreet ... clear ... measurable ... product. There is nobody ... NOBODY ... on this whole planet who can provide exactly what you provide. **YOU INC.** Doesn't it have a lovely ring to it?

Make a game of it: It's 6 a.m. **Marge Jacobsen, Inc.** rises from bed, has a cup of coffee (or three), drives to her International Headquarters. Marge Jacobsen, Inc., boots up her computer. MJ Inc. addresses her Several Publics in her own UNIQUE way via each and every e-mail she sends and responds to. MJ Inc. works on relationships. MJ Inc. schedules a lunch with an interesting source of information. MJ Inc. c-a-r-e-f-u-l-l-y considers her To Do List. (It is, after all, the Company's/MJ Inc.'s Agenda—and direction—for this precious day ahead.)

Etc.

T.T.D./Inc.-ing

1. How about privately beginning to refer to yourself and a couple of coworkers as Margery Martinez, Inc., and her pals ... Deborah (probably not "Debbie") Atkins, Inc. and Dolph Serrino, Inc. How does it feel? What does it mean? What sort of stuff would Margery Martinez, Inc., **not do** today that "Margie-in-accounting" might let herself be distracted by?

2. To Do Lists are Holy. Things change in the course of a day ... every day. But your To Do List is, in effect, the same as NBC's schedule of programs. It is what you intend for the day at Harold R. Simpson, Inc.,

Accountant-on-the-Rise, to stand for. Right? So take that To Do (*and To Don't!*) List extremely seriously. **Think like the Schedulers for the President of the United States.** Every moment...every micro-event... has a Message. Adds or detracts from your Brand Image. I.e.: Become your own, conscious Spin Doctor, Herald, Message Maker for ... Harold R. Simpson, Inc.

8.

The Nub

The one-person business is ... business as lifestyle—business as a statement about who you are and what you value.
—Claude Whitmyer, Salli Rasberry, Michael Phillips,
Running a One-Person Business

Love that**!**

* **WHO YOU A-R-E.**

* **WHAT YOU V-A-L-U-E.**

Mastery. Growth. Distinction. WOW Projects. Autonomy. Self-control. WHAT I VALUE. These are the staples of BrandYou-BrandMe/Me Inc./You & Co. (And, again: What a difference from Dilbert-ville!)

It's survival. True. But it's also—or more so—morality. WHAT YOU VALUE. Can you honestly say that yesterday's four meetings "at work" were about "Work You Value"... in Life? Think back. Hard. Through each of those meetings. Did you sleepwalk? Or did you make a distinct —and it could be very quiet!—contribution consistent with Big Things in This Life that You Value as a Unique

Individual? How would your yesterday stack up with the Physician's Rounds or the Parish Priest's Visitation Schedule?

Does this sound too grand? Hey … it is Your Life/Your Life's Work we're talking about here!

T.T.D./The Moral Core of Brand You

1. So … go through yesterday's meetings/agendas. Carefully. What do they say about you? Do they reflect—unmistakably—the "things you value"? Now let's look forward to tomorrow or the next full week. How—specifically!—can you begin to rejigger your schedule to better reflect The Things You Value as Joan- (or Bob)-as-Brand You?

2. Got a Mission Statement? If not, why not? How do you know what you value if you don't have a summary statement … of some sort? If you don't have such a summary doc, gingerly start—alone or with a couple of colleagues—to think carefully through this Values Bit. (Hint: It is of abiding importance.)

3. Again (sorry): **What you value is u-n-m-i-s-t-a-k-a-b-l-y reflected in (1) precisely how you spend your time, (2) the nature of each contribution at each meeting, (3) who exactly you hang with.** So: How's it look? Pick one item to alter in the next 24 hours.

9.

E.g.:

* A viable economic proposition, succinctly described

* A full quiver of service "products"

* A client obsession

* A "sales bias"

* A clear grasp of bookkeeping fundamentals (e.g., what's it cost you to "do business," even if you're still on someone else's payroll)

* A viable network of "subcontractors" to perform support services

The Nub

Consider this useful set of business skills from Claude Whitmyer et al. in *Running a One-Person Business*:

* **Trade Skill** ... understanding how you translate your talents into a viable economic proposition.

* **Market Focus** ... there's got to be a customer for your "it."

* **Select customers with care** ... you *are* your customers.

* **Master bookkeeping fundamentals.**

* **Focus on one business ... but offer a variety of services associated therewith.**

* **Upgrade your skills** ... constantly.

* **Explain yourself** ... in 35 words or less.

* **Sell yourself.**

* **Develop an emotional support system—** e.g., "planning buddies" with whom you meet regularly to discuss progress and pratfalls.

"Business skills" are liberating as Hell! (They—literally—make us free.)

Most of us—even if we're on someone's payroll—need to work on acquiring them. Consciously. Though I had two degrees in "business," I still recall with horror my early days after leaving McKinsey & Co. I didn't know what things cost. I didn't know invoicing formats. I was a lousy negotiator. (Even though it was my own prospective bread I was seeking to butter.) In retrospect, if I'd had my eyes opened earlier, I could've saved myself from a bushel of blunders.

T.T.D./Skills Portfolio I

1. Purchase <u>Whitmyer et al.'s *Running a One-Person Business.*</u> Make it the subject of informal (or not-so-informal) Study Sessions with a handful of colleagues. This isn't cheating your employer: **Improved one-person business skills rebound to the benefit of the services you "sell" in your Dept.**

2. Go through each of the items listed above. Set up a Self-Study Program for each one, or at least the two or three where you feel you are most deficient. (Rank yourself—quantitatively—on each of the attributes.) Consider an outside-the-company course in, say, Accounting Basics.

3. Big Deal I: **Consider an MBA.** I'm a longtime, vociferous critic of some of the MBA's deficiencies. But I've got one. And I'm glad I do. And if you are a 34-year-old looking at an uncertain future (it *is* uncertain … it's just a matter of your acknowledging it … if you haven't yet), think about a night MBA program.

4. Big Deal II: **Consider a departmental or job transfer—including a lateral or even downward move—that will put you into a better position to develop/exercise One-Person Business Skills.** This may sound nutty (a downward move?!), but there's method to my madness. You do want to be prepared when the Big Boot aims its steel toe your way, don't you? <u>Having basic business skills is integral to building Brand You.</u> You'll be a lot better prepared when the time comes to launch.

9a.

Per William Bridges in *Creating You & Co.*:

* *The marketing hat*

* *The product development hat*

* *The operations hat*

* *The customer service hat*

* *The sales hat*

* *The information management hat*

* *The time management hat*

* *The planning hat*

The Nub

This is a variation on the theme of No. 9 above: Call it ...**The Eight Hats of Brand You.** True, it is a rather daunting list. But as an effective/entrepreneurial professional service firm member ... on the Acctg. Dept. payroll or as Honcho of Me Inc....you really do have to be at least moderately adept at all eight.

Marketing: Your marketing "literature" has to be compelling. (Even if you're still on that payroll.) Your Packaging has to be Memorable (see No. 6 above). Your Strategy for approaching/serving Clients must be crystal clear.

Product Development: You offer needed services. (Products, that is.) And your product portfolio must be constantly upgraded…dramatically upon occasion. Stale is as big a problem for you as it is for Hewlett-Packard.

Operations: There's a business—you!—to be run. Superb reports to be prepared. Brilliant subcontractors to be discovered and used. The figures do need to add up at the end of the month. The trains have to run on time. Sloppy operations can undermine You Inc. very quickly.

Customer Service: P-l-e-a-s-e call it **C**lient **S**ervice. (See our *the Professional Service Firm50* for the difference between "customers" and "Clients." Hint: It's enormous. Psychologically, at least.) And be clear that Client Service is a daily—hourly!—top, explicit priority. (Again, as much if you're still on the payroll of the Purchasing Dept. as if you're truly CEO of Me Inc.)

Sales: Sell! **Sell!** Sell! Doing WOW Projects, on or off someone's payroll, is a Sales Game! (See also our *the Project50* for lots more on this.)

Information Management: Big terms like "information infrastructure" apply as much—or more—to the One-Person Shop as to the gajillion $$$$ corporation. Maybe it's a glorified term for filing systems, but I know that getting mine up and running—and turning the info system into a genuine strategic asset—was a very big deal when I started on my own, after leaving McKinsey & Co. Me Inc. can't escape the Computer Age. To the contrary, Brand You's reach is facilitated by the computer network; make sure your skills are up to (and way beyond!) snuff.

Time Management: None of us ever gets this "right." (There just are not enough hours in the day.) But we must perpetually obsess on it. In short: We are as f-o-c-u-s-e-d/strategically clear as our allocation of time is focused.

Planning: Who Am I? What are My Values? And how do I deliver this Project ... with my values in tact? On time, on budget ... and with my unique WOW? All important. And all requiring thoughtful, though not overly complex, planning exercises.

None of the Eight Hats can be glossed over! You must turn yourself into an eight-headed marvel. Of course some hats will fit better than others ... and it's the ones that don't fit that you have to concentrate on.

T.T.D./The Eight Hats of Brand You

1. **How about starting a fresh file on each of the Eight Hats?** (Now.) Start attending to each of these discrete tasks.

2. Each week, go through the Eight Hats as a checklist: What have you done about each one? What's planned next week? Also, consider a Quarterly Eight Hats Review.

Alone. The idea: Make sure that each Hat is the subject of your serious consideration.

3. Prepare a more or less formal Study Plan for each of the Eight Hats. That is: You've got to get smarter about each one.

10.

That's what Springfield Remanufacturing Corp. chief Jack Stack calls it.

Idea: **You must understand how money is made.**

You must master the Basic Economics of Brand You... even if you remain on someone's payroll. Top line: You must—clearly —understand the market value of your "product." Bottom line: You must understand what it costs to produce that value (e.g., a $2,000/month travel and phone tab).

The Nub

Brand Yous provide services. That's our "product." Products—from M&Ms to architectural design services —have Market Value. And costs associated therewith: travel, phones, copiers, report preparation, research services, etc. The equation:

Negotiated price − Costs = Profits.

I was lucky. I had a vivacious Mary Kay saleswoman working part-time for me in 1983. A prospective client called; with no guidance, she quoted a price for a seminar that was three times higher than anything I'd charged before. *In Search of Excellence* was hot … and the prospective client signed off. I learned a very important lesson from that Mary Kay saleswoman. Namely: Ask and ye may very well receive.

Pricing services: I do a lot of public speaking to big convention crowds. Following retirement, a Colin Powell or George Bush enters the speakers' market at a stratospheric fee level that raises the bar. All the rest of us increase our fees accordingly … and happily slide in under the newly Powell-raised ceiling.

When it comes to my books, agent Esther Newberg at International Creative Management works for months to structure the many intricacies of a "deal." (And intricacies there are; one wants to ask for a high sum … *and* simultaneously develop-maintain a trusting relationship with the publisher. No walk in the park.)

Thus prices are set in the services market. Your price, to some extent, is your salary. But that salary is a rather general measure of what "people like you" are getting paid; it's not necessarily an accurate indicator of the market value of the unique services you provide.

Thus you begin a finer-grained value assessment with a clear definition of your product. Next check out fees garnered by those who sell such services on the open market. This isn't necessarily easy, but it is always possible. (You should do this even if you plan—for now—to stay on a payroll.) A sense of product definition, in terms the marketplace understands, and product value is important…for all of us.

Next up, try to get a grip on costs. Not easy in Big Corp. world, where so many services—like making 66 copies of a report—are "free." But, again, begin the process of figuring out what it costs to produce a valuable service. Odds are you'll be unpleasantly surprised. Which is more or less the point of the exercise. (Remember that Operations Hat from 9a above!)

I'm not urging you to obsess on all this. I am urging you to get moving. To begin to grasp the Economic Fundamentals of the Service(s)-Product(s) you—Brand You —provide.

T.T.D./Grasping the Business Equation

1. Start with a clear, market-focused definition of your Product(s). If possible, work with some "real" professional service providers on this. (Cadge a couple of hours from your next door neighbor, the Brand Him CPA.)

2. Do some research—on the Web, in trade journals, at a trade show—on the pricing of comparable services.

3. Think about your **U**nique **E**conomic **P**roposition. (It is not too grand a term, any more than it is for a premier major-league middle reliever.) What makes your product distinct? How should it/could it be priced?

4. Begin to accumulate cost data. A file folder— paper or electronic—will do for starters. Be careful:

There are a bunch of hidden costs.(E.g., four hours of the services of a Graphic Arts specialist to format a report, if you're not a desktop publishing whiz yourself.)

5. Consider a very rough Profit & Loss Statement.(Or at least start keeping a rough log—lawyer-like—of Billable Hours.)

11.

GIVE THE WORLD A CLEAR PICTURE OF WHO YOU ARE.

Don't be glib. Figuring out "who you are" is a form of psychotherapy!

The Nub

Me. Tom. "I give speeches/seminars. I write books." Not very helpful, is it? "Management speeches"? A little better. "Seminars for managers on how to deal with workplace changes at the turn of the century"? Hackneyed … but at least a little more precise.

How about you: "Recognized expert, with more than 25 published articles, on the issue of how to avoid sexual harassment lawsuits in the workplace. Extensive experience in financial services and retail industries."
Clear. Precise. (If a little light on Pizzazz.)

You get the idea. I.e.:

* WHO ARE YOU?

* WHAT IS YOUR PRODUCT?

* HOW IS "IT" SPECIAL?

* HOW IS IT DIFFERENT FROM OTHERS' SIMILAR OFFERINGS?

* HOW CAN I DEMONSTRATE ITS TRUSTWORTHINESS?

* HOW CAN I DEMONSTRATE I'M "WITH IT"/ CONTEMPORARY?

* HOW CAN I DEMONSTRATE "COOL"?

These are garden-variety issues for the marketers at Frito-Lay or Gillette. And questions in a foreign tongue for the average trainer or IS specialist. Well, Ms. Brand You-to-be, time to learn that foreign tongue!

No surprise: The harder you work at this ... the bigger the payoff. In the world of branding, there are layers upon layers upon layers of meaning that get translated into the Lasting Value Proposition.

It combines for the likes of us: (1) a growing skill base (the stuff you know); (2) a proven track record (project implementation that sticks); (3) managed word-of-mouth reputation (client testimony, seminars conducted at local trade shows, your Web site); (4) Dressing for Success (how do you and your calling card look?); (5) speaking skills (join Toastmasters ... today); and (6) the elusive but all-important issue of character (in the end you are "selling" the Essence-of-You).

I'm trying to make this complicated. (Not the normal explainer's tactic.) Because it is complicated.

You—Brand You—are a mass of tangibles and intangibles—just like Coca-Cola. (Yes, Coca-Cola ... with over $150 billion in market capitalization. It sells sugar water.

And a feel. And a pause that refreshes. And security. And … and … a hundred billion dollars or so worth of "and" … "and"!)

So … start working on that Convincing-Cool-Distinct-Picture-of-You/Essence-of-You/Lasting-Value-Proposition. Today!

T.T.D. / Who E-x-a-c-t-l-y Are You?

1. Study "people brands." Martha Stewart. Oprah. Placido Domingo. Frank Gehry (the architect). Michael Jordan. Lee Iacocca. To what end? **To begin the Thinking Process surrounding People-as-Distinct-Product.**

2. *Don't* rush to a Product/Brand Statement. *Do* start jotting down notes. Words. Phrases. That fit you. The person. Your product. Your skills. Your attitude. Your character.

3. At some point, when your comfort level with who you are is high, rough out a formal Marketing Brochure. Continue to refine. Forever.

4. Work alone. Work with others. Make friends with a professional or two at a local ad or PR agency.

5. Volunteer for a community fund-raising drive you care about. Look at how a clear "selling proposition" is formed. (My wife's business marketing skills were formed by leading a five-year community fund-raising effort to build a major ice rink and performing arts center in southern Vermont.)

12.

Change: Consulting Director to ... *Catalyst for Revolution.* CIO/Chief Information Officer to ... CEFRNS/**Chief Evangelist For Really Neat Stuff.** (Etc.)

The Nub

I've been pounding on you pretty hard. All the things you've got to do. Brand like Coca-Cola. Account like Arthur Andersen. Sell like Zig Ziglar.

So let's lighten up ... and let the fun begin! You are Ms. Cool. Right? Revolutionary-in-Waiting? WOW Projects Princess?

Outrageously Committed?

Well, put "it" ... your marvelous madcap moniker ... on your calling card. Time to pick a title. Think about these:

* *King of Kool Kapers*
* *Revolutionary*
* *Out of the Closet Revolutionary*
* *Change Champion*
* *Zest Zealot*

* *Grand Panjandrum of Pandemonium*
* *Passion Pilot*
* *WOW!Projects Hound*
* *WOW!Thing*
* *Wizard of WOW!*
* *Chief Evangelist for Really Neat (Cool) (Rockin') (Amazing) (Fantabulous) Stuff*
* *Raging Inexorable Thunderlizard Evangelist*
* *Catalyst for Revolution*
* *Mistress of Madness*
* *Client Service Maniac*
* *Producer of Impossible Dreams*
* *Rocker of Boats*
* *Disturber of the Peace*
* *Unrepentant Rebel*
* *Chief Freak.*
* *Supreme Shit Stirrer*

Several of these titles—including Raging Inexorable Thunderlizard Evangelist—are real. (R.I.T.E. was marketing guru Guy Kawasaki's self-granted title on the original Apple Macintosh computer development team.)

My (v-e-r-y) serious point: Brand Yous—as I see them —are out to Change the World. To Raise a Little (Lotta)

Hell. To do Work That Matters. So ... why not a strong (and perhaps funky/somewhat outrageous) job title that makes your case in five words or less?

T.T.D./Thunderlizard Evangelism!

1. This is done best over a beer or chardonnay. With some pals. Jump-start your Brand You Identity Quest by playing with names. Follow standard brainstorming rules. No negatives. The more outrageous the better. Go for broke ... no holds barred ... no inhibitions allowed. (Prune the list later.)

2. Take your time. It's Your Identity we're talking about!

3. Using *Fast Company* magazine and the like, start "researching" Strong/Cool job titles. (*Fast Company* has a few zany ones in each issue.)

4. Eventually ... take the plunge. *At least with an alternative set of business cards you can use when you feel comfortable/outrageous.*

5. Hey, this—Brand You—**is** an Adventure. Let's make it a Hoot/Blast. (P.S.: It's So Serious, it ought to be fun.) (P.P.S.: Humor is an awesome and underused business tool.)

13.

We must become the change we want to see in the world.
—Gandhi

The Nub

Several of these points have (appropriately) focused on…WHO AM I? I've long had a simple answer to the "Who am I?" question:

Y-O-U A-R-E Y-O-U-R C-A-L-E-N-D-A-R!

The "secret" to success in taking on the Quality Issue in 1985? Going to a Deming seminar? Studying Crosby? Sure…but…NO. The (real) secret: Spending 50 percent of your most precious asset—your time!—on Quality per se.

Call it Walk the Talk or Talk the Walk. Call it You Must Be the Change You Wish to See. Call it…

Attention Is All There Is.

Or follow Texas Bix Bender: "A body can pretend to care, but they can't pretend to be there."

If Brand You is about your Signature WOW Projects ... and it is ... then you must somehow (consult the Time Management gurus) weed out the 96(!) percent of distractions ... and Work-the-Hell-Out-of-Your-Signature-WOW Project (come Bloody Hell and Bloody High Water). We all know folks who are going to ... start a business ... write a book ... learn to skydive ... build a house ... as soon as they "find the time." **BULLSHIT!** When you CARE you MAKE the time ... and if that means saying "NO!" to your friends, your spouse, your kids (hey, I never said there would be no sacrifices), well, there it is!

(When I'm at work on a book—i.e., now—I am unspeakably rude to friends, family, colleagues. Sometimes correspondence goes unanswered for a ... year. And far too many Little League games have been missed. And Mom has gone far too long without a phone call. Etc. Fact is: I don't know how else to do it?! And there may well be no other way?)

TIME!

It's hackneyed: But "it" is all we have. I went on some errands early this morning. Two of the stores I stopped at were not open ... though their published hours said they were supposed to be. I was furious. (Far more furious than the "little" lapse demanded.) But I'm writing a damn book! (Actually ... three.) T-I-M-E! It's a-l-l I've got. (A-L-L: **DO YOU UNDERSTAND?**) Brand You = Time *Consciousness*. Brand You = Time *Fetish*. Brand You = *Obsession* with Time.

I-T I-S A-L-L I/Y-O-U H-A-V-E. (A lost day ... a lost hour! ... is just that ... **L-O-S-T**. Carpe diem ... 'cause if you don't carpe it, the diem is gone ... forever.)

T.T.D./Attention Is All There Is!

1. Become—and start today, damn it!—Obsessive about Your Calendar/To Do List. **Examine it microscopically *each* morning. Do a postmortem *each* night.** Does it reflect—**exactly!**—your one or two or three (no more!) Brand You priorities?

2. Form a Calendar Support Group ... with three or four fellow Brand You Wannabes. (NO KIDDING.) Have an AA-like weekly Calendar Review Session. Keep each other on track/message/focus!

3. Weed the B.S. D-a-i-l-y.

4. Turn unweedable B.S. into Opportunities Consistent with Your Brand You Prospectus/Manifesto/Objectives. Key idea: How do I convert this d-r-e-a-r-y task into Something Cool? Hint: It can always be done. (See our *the Project50*.)

14.

Here's some terrific advice for Change Agents from former USWest exec Bob Knowling:

* We all have some space. Start with things within your purview.

* Asking for permission is asking to be told "no."

* The system is stacked against you. Pick your battles.

* You have to have a model/concept: "What's my point of view?"

* Politics is life: A dead change agent doesn't do anybody any good.

* Change agentry isn't mainly about the issues. It's about moving people out of their comfort zones.

The Nub

We've talked about the sexy side of Brand You: What do I want to be? Etc. And that's what we should have done.

Now to the … sweaty side. Or rather, now to …

I-M-P-L-E-M-E-N-T-A-T-I-O-N.

A.k.a. politics! Politics is usefully defined as "the art of getting things done" or "the art of the possible." All of life is political. It's well nigh impossible to accomplish WOW (that sticks!) alone. Therefore, it's to your profound advantage to master the Art of Politics (in the best sense of the word—i.e., cooperation and compromise in pursuit of a goal). And if you love—or learn to embrace/love—politics, odds go way up that you'll make a Good/Great Change Agent—and a notable Brand You. If you can't bring yourself to Embrace Politics, more's the pity. (I.e.: Forget making a difference. Truly. S-o-r-r-y.)

But back a step to the main point here: You are N-E-V-E-R helpless. (**Unless** … you define yourself so.) Any task—see No. 15 below and our *the Project50*—can be turned into a Worthy/Cool Pursuit. It's all a matter of attitude! The (li'l) Spring Office Cleanup can be transformed into the equivalent of baseball's Spring Training: A Perfect Moment for Reassessment and Rebirth. E.g.: *How do we make the l-o-o-k and f-e-e-l of the office reflect our New-WOW!-Cool-Pugnacious-Revolutionary Spirit?*

Bob Knowling, above, offers other gems. It's hackneyed: ASKING FOR PERMISSION IS ASKING TO BE TOLD NO. But it also happens to be … Gospel Truth. And too often honored—age 23 or age 53—in the breach. (Ever heard of a Real Revolutionary—the kind who makes it into your kid's tenth-grade history book—who "asked

permission"? E.g.: G. Washington? M.L. King, Jr.? Coperni-
cus? Admiral Hyman Rickover, father of the nuclear
Navy?)

We've got a whole book coming up on the topic: *the
Power+Implementation50*. Meanwhile, I'll just repeat:
"POLITICS" IS **N-O-T** A DIRTY WORD. POLITICS IS LIFE!
(If you plan to get real-WOW stuff done.)

T.T.D./Implementation Fanaticism = Embracing Politics!

1. Talk about "politics" with two or three trusted
colleagues. TALK TO A PAL WHO'S A STATE LEGISLATOR.
Talk about V-i-r-t-u-e. *And* the reality of Implementation.

2. Have an informal session with three or four Brand
You Hopefuls. Go through the Bob Knowling list above.
**Discuss the application of each of Knowling's
ideas to your current project(s).** Don't stop
until you have come up with an action plan for testing/
implementing at least one of the Knowling ideas.

3. Start a library of Power+Implementation books.
Invite your division's most effective Project Manager in
to talk to you and your colleagues about her implementation tricks of the trade.

15.

Seek independence. Make your own jurisdiction. Golden Rule: Any-Damn-Task-Can-Be-Turned-to-Gold ... with Imagination. (Don't let on, but this is key: You don't need the "great"/"big" project.) (Trust me. Please: *In Search of Excellence* emerged from a project in which no one put any faith ... or initial resources.) It's the "little," "unwanted" job—SHAPE UP OUR RELATIONSHIPS WITH A FEW MINOR VENDORS WHO ARE OUT OF SORTS—that can literally unlock Pandora's WOW!/Profitable Box.

The Nub

So how do you ... age 26 and low on the Totem Pole ... make a project, any damn project, C-o-o-l?

Well ... you do. You can. You will. (And speaking of will, it's the most important ingredient of all.)

You take on a little project at church to work with preschoolers. Four years later, you're in the White House being celebrated for your imaginative Preschool Program ... that the Most Powerful Human on Earth (U.S. Pres.) wants to take nationwide.

These things do happen.

And the Seriously Cool Ones invariably start from Innocent/Small/Wee Beginnings. (Yes: invariably!) Papers to mark the hymns to be sung fell out of his hymnal. An itch (little) to be scratched. Voilà (15 or so years later): a billion $$$ Post-it product line for 3M.

A "little" client calls your training company. She wants her four service reps trained for ... a day. (You are Low Woman on the Totem Pole ... and you take the call. Hey, who else; it's "just" a tiny client.) But you have a g-r-e-a-t chat with her. She really wants to Shoot the Moon. You "shouldn't" (officially), but you invest day-after-day-after-day researching her project. You create a truly original workshop. Two years later, that workshop and its spin-offs have become 35 percent of your company's business. You're a VP at age 28.

It is all a matter of a-t-t-i-t-u-d-e. Crappy assignment? Or Opportunity No. 1? (No one's watching ... precisely because it's a "crappy assignment.")

Sorry. You're reading the wrong guy's book. I don't subscribe to power-less-ness**!** The Word according to Roseanne: <u>Nobody gives you power. You must take it.</u> And I'd add: age 26. Or 66. Or age 16 to age 86, perhaps.

T.T.D./Volunteer for Rotten Jobs!

1. Next time a "crappy" "little" task pops up ... take it. Gleefully. Redefine it.

Make it **OH SO C-O-O-L.** In fact, don't wait for a crappy little task to slither into your lap. Seek one out**!** Today**!**

2. See No. 1 above. Repeat. Regularly.

3. Find a couple of co-conspirators/Brand You Trainees: Work together on reformulating a "small" project to send a "big" message. Work meticulously on this. Forge a ... Portfolio of Way Cool Projects from Sows' Ears.

4. Small Task = **B-I-G** Opportunity. Talk about it with a few of your peers ... a respected elder advisor. **Don't e-v-e-r accept "small" as a "given."**

15a.

John Wooden, the legendary basketball coach:

"We get distracted by what is outside our control. ... [Success] begins by trying to make each day count. ... If you sincerely try to make each day a masterpiece, angels can do no better."

I once labeled it "One Minute Excellence." I stole the idea from the legendary IBM boss Tom Watson, not Ken Blanchard. Asked how to achieve excellence, Mr. Watson replied, and I paraphrase slightly: "Quit doing nonexcellent stuff." My version: Quit doing nonexcellent stuff. It's Brand You Time: You—and you alone!—are ultimately responsible for the way in which today's activities enhance —or detract from—your emergent track record.

The Nub

I'd really prefer not to sound like EST-man Werner Erhard (or Tony Robbins). But I really do agree with Mr. Watson of IBM (who sounds like Erhard and Robbins): **THE PATH TO EXCELLENCE IS TO HALT— NOW!—ALL UN-EXCELLENT STUFF.**

It is that simple. It is that hard. **Cut the Crap = Step No. 1 toward Excellence + Brand You.**

Question:

Not ... can you do it? (Hint: Yes, you can!)

But ... **will you do it?**

Starting with ... your next project-team meeting? (Twenty minutes from now.)

Starting with ... today's To Do List.

Again: The whole damn idea of this book—of this series of books—is taking our lives back from "them" ... Faceless Big Corp.'s Mindless Hierarchy. Becoming responsible for the WOW!-in-Our-Projects-and-Professional-Lives. Just saying/shouting "No" to the Dilbert-ization of work.

* * *

A colleague was under horrid deadline pressure. As he rushed out of the office, he ran past me, the proposal for a project still virtually damp with ink.

It was a shitty thing to do, I know. But I did it. I said, "Hey, is it [proposal] WOW!?" [I HAVE TAUGHT MYSELF TO AUTOMATICALLY ASK THAT QUESTION.]

"We'll talk when I get back," he said.

"No, we'll talk now," I said.

"Huh?"

"Now."

He at least slowed down. [I'm sorta his boss, but I'm also not really in the chain of command.]

"Why not postpone the meeting," I asked, "until you can get to WOW! or at least close?"

Now he did stop. And we had a five-minute chat. (Well, three.) And he didn't postpone the meeting. (I told you I had no real power.) But he did agree to reframe it with the client, as a "draft" rather than a "final" proposal. He agreed to tell the client that neither he nor they should move forward until they at least agreed on the specifics of a "WOW! Outcome."

Life is always "on deadline." So ... WOW! Now. Or ... more or less ... Never.

Okay?

T.T.D./ WOW Now!

1. Look at today's To Do List. Now. Is there non-WOW! on it? If so, how do you **(1)** WOW! it, **(2)** postpone it, or **(3)** drop it? **(Seriously.)**

2. YOU (Prospective Brand You that you are! Right?) learn to ask of yourself/others: "Is it WOW!? If not ... Stop."

Motto. As of Now:

"100 percent 'Braggable' Work!"

Okay? (If not, explain why not ... to yourself and to your spouse/significant other ... and to your closest friend ... and your Mom.)

* * *

WEED OUT NON-WOW!

NOW!

16.

From UPS to Marriott, most of the companies we most admire were founded on a shoestring. Literally: Less than a coupla thousand bucks.

You don't need a silver (corporate or personal) spoon to sally forth. You do need passion, commitment, a few pals ... and a **Consuming Desire** to take the next, usually wee step.

The Nub

The implicit theme of items No. 14 through No. 16 is ...

NO EXCUSES:

* You *do* have "space."

* You *don't* need "permission."

* You *don't* need "power."

* You *don't* need a "big" task.

* You *don't* need money.

Money kills. (Or at least it can.) With big bucks, you're too soon beholden to the funder ... which can prevent us from taking the truly WOW leaps. But mostly, history is on your (poverty-stricken) side. Most cool stuff—products and companies and revolutions—was started in basements and garages, for (literal) pennies. Sony. UPS. Marriott. Apple. HP. Pizza Hut. Microsoft. FedEx. Etc.

(Consider: Imagine Gandhi's budget. He merely created Earth's Largest Democracy.)

If you don't have $$$$, you're forced to ... find Friends. An expert pal who will lend you some time. (The resource that really counts!) A Wacky Customer who will let you test your stuff at her place. Necessity *is* the Mother of Invention, and it is also the Mother of a Cool Network of Volunteer Fellow Pirates-Revolutionaries. Network Building beats $$$$. Any time. (Mostly.) Money fosters bloat, waste, complacency. It's the enemy of resourcefulness, grit, drive. Hunger (of all kinds) is the great motivator.

T.T.D./Scrounge!

1. Scrounging = Networking Mentality. So ... start Scrounging/Networking. In the next ten working days, schedule **3** breakfasts and **4** lunches (yes, I am being precise/quantitative) with would-be volunteers/supporters for your In-the-Making-WOW!-Project.

2. Treat your Project like an NPR-PBS fund-raising drive. I.e.: Think ... recruitment of volunteers.

17.

Starting today: Always think—obsess!—on your portfolio of accumulating project work.

ALL WORK THAT "COUNTS" TOWARD BRAND YOU BECOMES DISCRETE, CLIENT-CENTRIC, WOW PROJECT WORK. "It" is the currency of Brand You. "It" is your (only?) ticket to liberation (on or off somebody's payroll) and psychological/real independence.

The Nub

(1) Forget "tasks." **(2)** E-m-b-r-a-c-e Projects. **(3)** Think ... **PORTFOLIO** ... of projects.

I simply want to up the decibel count here. Recall:

I AM MY PROJECTS.

(And y-e-s, it does bear repeating. Too many ... still ... just Don't Seem to Get It.)

The bigger idea (here):

Brand You = Project Portfolio, **Coolness Thereof.** Period. (P-E-R-I-O-D.)

Redux redux:

I-AM-MY-PROJECT-PORTFOLIO. AND THE COOLNESS-BEAUTY-BOLDNESS THEREOF. (Or n-o-t.)

Project. Portfolio. **Currency.** Signature. It's w-h-a-t I a-m.

I've had good projects. One **g-r-e-a-t** project. (It led to *In Search of Excellence*.) Mediocre projects. And b-o-m-b-s.

No matter. Projects all! Portfolio entries all! The bridges—about four—I built in Vietnam in 1966–1968. And the gun emplacement I built in Vietnam, which got written up in an engineering magazine. And the Pentagon project that led to the Navy base on Diego Garcia in the Indian Ocean. And the opium eradication project in Mexico that I spearheaded during a White House/OMB/State Department stint in 1973–74.

Etc.

Etc.

Project. Project. Project.

Project**s**. Project**s**. Project**s**.

I carry them around. Figuratively. And literally.

I gave a speech 43 hours before writing this. To the Midwest Beauty Show. (No beauty I! Understatement!) Some 500 folks … mostly owners of Hair Salons. Cool

Folks. In charge of their lives! Making a difference in their Clients' lives!

The speech was a … p-r-o-j-e-c-t. I'm 56. Been doing what I've been doing for 30 years or so. Brought every iota of energy and intelligence and emotion to bear on that 2-hour speech.

It's … "another" … project. Yup. And: My … T-O-T-A-L … signature … as a Human Being … for that day (2/27/99). It's what I f-e-e-l as I walk onstage … at the Midwest Beauty Show: I'll make … or blow! … My Whole Damn Bloody Life in the next 120 m-i-n-u-t-e-s. One hundred and twenty minutes. Seven thousand two hundred seconds. To make a d-i-f-f-e-r-e-n-c-e in 500 lives. **Or not.**

Y-i-k-e-s.

(Oh shit.)

Projects! I love 'em … and they scare the bejesus out of me. (When they stop scaring me, I'll be REALLY scared.) They are me.

T.T.D./ (Project) Portfolio Quality!

1. Brand You = Your **Portfolio** of Projects. So: Begin by making a list of recent projects. (Last two years?) Assess each project and the whole list on several dimensions (characteristics of the ideal portfolio): riskiness, impact, beauty (yes!), implementation effectiveness, Client raves, etc. Does the Portfolio add up to something of unusual distinction? Where are the holes? (E.g., not many daring adventures, too many implementation shortfalls.) If the Portfolio is not all it might be to you as a prospective Brand You, what can you do—with, say, your current project—to start to fill in the blanks? What can you do about an upcoming assignment to twist it in a more useful direction?

2. If you're boss, work explicitly with each professional on the shape of her or his Portfolio. Use the term! (Portfolio.) Make sure that each assignment amounts to an explicit effort to improve each team member's Project Portfolio—to, say, fill in a hole or two. Use Project Portfolio Assessment as a/the centerpiece of Annual Evaluations.

17a.

YOU ARE THE "WOW!-NESS" | OF EVERY PROJECT.

So ... **up the formal WOW! Score of every project.** Try this ritual:

1. *Make a list* of current projects.

2. *Describe* the attributes of a WOW! Outcome for each one (for you, for the Client).

3. *Rank* projects on **(1)** your Passion for each one, **(2)** WOW!-ness of outcome.

4. *Pick* one project with High Passion, High WOW!

5. Do a rough draft—one-page max.—*revised description* of the project that emphasizes the WOW!; shop it around with a customer, some close pals.

6. Reduce the one-page *"project sell document"* to five bullet points that can be fit on a 5 x 7-inch index card.

7. *Proceed* toward execution … never letting the WOW! slip into the background.

Simple message: *You're not going to create WOW! Projects and WOW Portfolios of Projects unless you're willing to talk—explicitly—about WOW!*

The Nub

1. I *AM* MY PROJECTS.

2. I *AM* MY PROJECT PORTFOLIO … AGE 16 TO 76.

3. *I AM THE "WOW!-SCORE" OF EACH—AND EVERY—PROJECT IN MY PORTFOLIO.*

4. P-E-R-I-O-D.

If the Project/Portfolio is not Cool …

You Are Not Cool. Period. If the Project Portfolio doesn't Rock …

You Do Not Rock. Period.

T.T.D. / WOW!-Score

1. Measure. **Measure.** Measure.

That is: **Score the "WOW!"** on your current-prospective project(s). How? Ask yourself. Ask your team-mates. Ask the Client. Ask an outsider. Ask them to score —scale of 1 ("same old same old") to 10 ("takes my breath away with its audacity")—the current incarnation of the project. They can. (We've asked this in our training programs a hundred times: An ensuing, invariably rich discussion occurs over "What's 'WOW'?" and "What's the difference between a score of 4 and a score of 6?" That discussion is the point!)

2. Reframe **The Project** until you get the WOW! Score Up-**Up-Up.** Again, work with various interested parties.

3. Iron Law: Use "the word." WOW! Constantly. Make it second nature.

18.

It's easy to decide what you're going to do. The hard thing is deciding what you're not going to do.

—Michael Dell

The Nub

Clarity of focus.

D-e-m-o-n-i-c focus.

Strong terms. Justified. <u>Brand You Sin No. 1: Dispersion of Energy</u>!

Nike does a lot of stuff … now. It started with shoes. Period. Levi's does a lot of stuff … now. It started with riveted jeans. Period. Michael Jordan had some trouble with baseball. I don't tango very well. Etc.

I.e.: <u>Brand You = Distinction = Implementation =</u>
<u>D-e-m-o-n-i-c Focus.</u>

To which you rebut, "But I've got a dozen different things on my agenda." Yes … b-u-t. First, I bet you can find a way to dump three-quarters of them. (Practice Strategic Rudeness. Better rude … and f-o-c-u-s-e-d … than polite and scattered/indistinct.) Second, take the two or three items that remain … and twist each one until it intensifies your quintessential Brand You Profile.

*Then … hold on to your hat … prune some more. The magic-Number-is-**1**. All this is brutally hard work. But it's worth the candle. Because: You haven't got a candle unless you focus. But it's also exciting … exhilarating … thrilling … a total HIGH … to really bring all your personal resources to bear … to really concentrate everything you've got … on* **a** *project. I.e.: You suddenly look up and three (five? eight?) hours—or days!—have flown by … and during that time you have made a decisive step toward memorable Brand You.*

So:

1. Take a good time-management course.

2. Consult with a time-management advisor quarterly.

3. List everything you've done in the last week. Put priorities on each item—relative to your Brand You Distinctive Competence. Whack 25 percent to 75(!) percent off the list. Re-plan this week's calendar accordingly.

4. Form a "Cut the Bullshit" Calendar Support Group. Help one another keep focused. Make it fun!

5. Don't respond to stupid e-mail.

6. Cut your number of meetings attended by one-third.

7. Work at home one day a week. (Or at the nearby park or Starbucks.)

8. Teach yourself to say "No." THIS IS HARD FOR MANY OF US. (E.G., ME!) Because it's hard, you (I) must consciously practice. (E.g., stand in front of a mirror and repeat **"no"** 25 times. I actually do this upon occasion.)

9. Enlist your boss if possible. Chat with her about your Brand You Aspirations (a good deal for her ... because you intend to pursue excellence at something of importance). Share your plans—lightheartedly—of future Strategic Rudeness; make her an ally.

10. Think about the AA model: One Day at a Time. Like stopping booze, cigarettes, or whatever, this (demonic focus) is an hour-by-hour struggle.

T.T.D./Focus = O-N-E

1. Review the list immediately above. GET TO WORK.

2. Are you clear: What is the **o-n-e** thing you want to be distinct for/at? (In a big way.) Describe it ... *carefully.* Write it down. Pin it above your desk. Put it on your screen saver. Carry it on a card in your wallet. Explain it—in 25 words or less—to anyone whose path you cross (that includes the checkout person in the supermarket).

3. Assuming you've got at least a tentative answer to No. 2 above ... swear to me (swear to yourself, is more like it) that 75 percent of your (precious) time will be focused —**somehow or other**—on that o-n-e measure/dimension of your true distinction.

4. Consider taking a course in meditation ... a yoga class ... a painting class ... anything that builds your concentration ... that empties your mind of clutter ... that helps you attain the state of grace needed to really focus all your energies on your signature project(s).

* * *

CLUTTER KILLS WOW!

19.

I.e.: The project can be only as good (WOW!) as your ability to embark on a Daring Adventure **with** your Client. So choose—and reject—Clients with the utmost care. Yes, you do have the power to choose … and to reject. Life (Brand You Life) = Choice. Or else. (Or else you ain't on the road to True Distinction.)

The Nub

Brand You = Client-centric Life.

You (Brand You) = Your Client Portfolio.

Okay, I said it before (several times!):

I AM MY PROJECTS.

Now I'm adding the Second Half of the Message:

I **AM** MY CLIENTS!

That is … professionally … I **am** those whom I serve.

Okay?

It's pretty easy to write this. It's well nigh impossible to convey the profound meaning. Ask me what I "do," and

I guess I'll tell you I "lecture on management." In the next breath, I'll say I've talked to IBM, Sun, PeopleSoft, Allstate … and the independent salon entrepreneurs at the Midwest Beauty Show … in the last six months. That is, I am professionally defined by those with whom I do business.

Yes … **defined.**

It's as obvious as the end of your nose … when we're talking about who your 14-year-old hangs out with. And it should be equally obvious when it comes to your Client List.

I could go on … and on. (And I do in our *the Professional Service Firm50.*) I'm who I *do* hang with. *And* who I *don't* hang with. (And I fervently believe that bigness achieved by acquiring dreary Clients is a losing proposition of the first order.)

T.T.D./You = Your Clients

1. *C*-l-i-e-n-t. Use that word. Always capitalize it. **Period.**

2. It's natural—if not laudatory—to angle for the "in" party invitations. (It's High Art in Washington, D.C.) Well … Client Selection is the Same Game. We are known by our Portfolio of Clients. Admit it. And: M-a-n-a-g-e to it.

3. WE SERVE CLIENTS. IT'S WHAT WE DO. IT'S WHAT **I**—AS BRAND YOU—DO.

PERIOD. (Post these words above your desk. Or some such.)

4. So make your Client List count. Alone—or with a few others—assess the strengths and weaknesses of each Client: **(1)** What can I learn from them? **(2)** Are they trustworthy? **(3)** Will they "joint venture" with me on interesting projects? Treat me as a learning partner? **(4)** Are they innovators? Willing to take risks? **(5)** Will they force me to stretch, challenge me, never settle for less than WOW!?

5. Use your evaluations (No. 4 above) as the basis for a systematic plan for approaching/reapproaching every Client. Work with each priority Client on a Future Work Strategy. Make the process formal. Make the aim no less than **100%** WOW Work.

20.

Scarf up feedback.

Become a Client satisfaction fanatic.

Make user-friendliness a mainstay of every project. (Consciously. EVERY DAY.)

The Nub

Alas, the average "staffer" is...**not**...a "Client Feed-back Fanatic." And...alas...that's an understatement.

True (B-I-G I-D-E-A) ... you must lead your Client to The Promised Land. But you also must be **Ms.(Mr.) Empathy.**

Can you "lead" and "suck up" at the same time? In a world-class way? Absolutely! I, for one, pride myself ... equally! ... on both. (And worry ... equally! ... about both.) I want to make an impact. (Lead.) But I want to do so with total empathy. (Listen.)

If you don't care ... if you don't want to help ... *desperately* ... you shouldn't be in "our"—Brand You—business. **We—you and me—are in a Helping Profession** ... as much as an ER nurse.

I think I'm pretty damn good at what I do. But it doesn't matter—a whit!—unless I can connect.

C-O-N-N-E-C-T.

(Hey, I beat people up for a living. I S-T-R-E-T-C-H T-H-E-M T-O T-H-E B-R-E-A-K-I-N-G P-O-I-N-T. Including, I hope, you. But I get away with it only because I do care. If you don't care … **in a big, personal way** … you're not worth my time. Really. And sorry.)

Brand You = Caring

Brand You = Helping

Brand You = Empathy

Brand You = Listening

T.T.D./Empathy!

1. This one is tough. As tough as any item on the *50List*. If the client is an "idiot" who "just doesn't get it"; and you're a "long-suffering genius" … you are d-o-o-m-e-d. (And I have seen it a hundred times. Or more. Message: Smart alecks finish last. Smart alecks make for rotten Brand Yous.)

Ours (Professional Services) is an Empathy/Helping/ Listening Business. We do have unique skills. (Or we shouldn't be practicing in the first place.) But we **Make a Difference** only to the extent that we **Connect** … as Empathetic/Helping Professionals-Humans. Think about it. Talk about it with two or three close colleagues.

It is—no baloney!—the Essence of Brand You. (**Real brands connect.** Right? On an emotional level. Right? Emotional connection is the heart and soul of branding—almonds or architecture. Right?)

2. Have a "Sit-down" with each of your Clients. A de facto psychotherapeutic session:

Am I—really?!—Connecting?

I do want to lead you, provoke you (in the best sense), but I want also to be your **F**ull **E**motional **P**artner in the **D**ramatic **C**hange **P**rocess that these **I**nsane **T**imes **D**emand.

3. Make the "Sit-down" the beginning of a carefully tended process of working with each Client—formally and regularly—to constantly ensure that "I'm Getting It." (Again: This doesn't happen by accident!)

4. Consider some formal training in Empathetic Listening. (Or even some coursework in Clinical Psychology.)

5. Think about trust. (We trust the brands we love ... trust them to deliver time and time again.) Talk with the Client. It can be a difficult conversation. But useful. And if it goes nowhere, what does it say about the Client? Or, heaven forbid, you?

Talk ... *immediately* ... about any real or perceived breach of trust. Consider trust-building exercises.

21.

Your/our "skill package" must be no less than ... **stunning.**

The Nub

You've simply got to know a lot about something of significant value to a bunch of Potential Clients. Bottom line: No discernibly **saleable** skills = No luck at Brand You-ing it.

S-A-L-E-A-B-L-E. D-I-S-T-I-N-C-T-I-O-N. It should hardly come as a surprise. Saleable Distinction is, after all, what a brand is. Morton Salt. Saran Wrap. The Lady Sensor. So what are **you** ... *exceptionally* ... *memorably* ... "good at"? That's worth purchasing?

Fair question.

Eh?

We can't all be "great." Can't all glide like Michael Jordan. Or empathize like Oprah Winfrey. But we ... **can** ... aspire ... to achieve ... distinction ... of some sort. About something of value.

Brand You = Saleable Distinction.

(Just keep telling yourself this. Every **moment**. Every **day**. Every **meeting**. Every **project**. Saleable Distinction … **OR ELSE**. There's no escaping this. No avoiding it. Revisit the basic logic: 90+ percent of our currently configured White Collar Jobs are in … jeopardy. In the next ten years. It's no game.)

My point: Your/My life is at stake here. So look at yourself and your skills/talents/potential … with brutal honesty. You probably have more (a lot more) to offer than you realize. So …

Focus on the **one** area where you are most capable of creating true, saleable distinction. Then … go for it! (Take **one** action today to polish-pronounce-"advertise" that distinction.

T.T.D./Vive La (Valued) Différence!

1. So … **how am I different?** In ways that are … of value? (Not "Michael Jordan different" … but on my way to achieving some noticeable distinction.) Be precise. Very precise.

2. **Are you sure?** Saleable Distinction is a Huge Phrase. Think about it/you. Do you have a truly **O**riginal **V**oice? A clear **P**oint **O**f **V**iew? Some **I**deas **Y**ou **C**are **D**eeply **A**bout that you'd like to turn into reality? Is your Sphere of Distinction one of **C**lear + **U**nmistakable **V**alue to **C**lients? If not … what is one step that you can take … right now … to shift the emphasis of your work on your

current project ... to help develop that Distinct + Saleable Voice? An Outcome That Matters and is of Value?

3. **Being "damn good" and "useful" is not even enough. Winners—today— must Stand for Something Important.** (Redux: Think about it. Talk with close colleagues about it.) What does Stand for Something Important mean? In 2000? In 2001? (And again: What can you do ... on Today's Project ... to reframe the task into one that helps you travel down this road?)

22.

Brand You is personal. But it's not a loner's world.

Brand You is a Team Sport!

You'll succeed to the extent that you work on creating "Tom's World" (or Mary's World ... or Dave's World). You must—consciously—think about your contacts list, both breadth and depth.

Concoct your own universe! This can happen inside the organization. ("Make your own McKinsey" was the brilliant advice one of my early McKinsey & Co. bosses gave me.) Or it can happen beyond the borders of your current organizational world, even if you choose to stay on the payroll ... for now.

The Nub

I could lose my luggage. Pain. No big deal. I could lose my wallet. Big Pain. No big deal. I could lose this manuscript. Huge pain. Big deal. Survivable.

But if I lost my Rolodex ... I might consider hari-kari. Seriously. (Almost.)

Brand You = Vital Growing Community of Useful/Supportive Contacts.

The big/**b-i-g** ideas:

* Community

* Management

* Maintenance

* Growth

* Systemization

* Attention

* Care

* Mutual Support

* Learning

* Feeding

* Trust

Brand You = Me Inc. "Inc.s" have suppliers and subcontractors ... and distributors and customer/Clients. The "Corporate Rolodex," if you will, is Life Itself. Me Inc. is an organism. An ecosystem. Growing. Or starving.

Mostly: The organism/ecosystem must be fed. Just like the garden.

"Get Rolodex Conscious," as one superstar networker said to me.

1. Organize-the-bloody-Hell-out-of-your-Rolodex.

NOW. (DAMN IT.) (Or at least start ... now.) Carefully choose your software—Microsoft Outlook, ACT!—or whatever.

2. Develop a simple but comprehensive system. But a system. (!) Categorize contacts. Note your last correspondence—e- or snail—to them. Record all sorts of items about them ... professional ... and personal.

3. Carefully review the entire Rolodex. At least monthly. Score each important or potentially important entry: Have I kept up with Mary? (1 = Hopeless neglect. 10 = Absolutely.)

4. Consciously tie the Rolodex to your Calendar. *Every* **breakfast and** *every* **lunch is a Rolodex Enhancement Opportunity.** Sound Machiavellian? Manipulative? It is!

This is ... **Your** Community.

Your Business Community.

Your Resources.

Your Clients.

Your Life.

Take it … seriously … and … systematically. (And be prepared to give twice what you take!)

5. Manage your Rolodex-Community **daily.** (No kidding.) Set aside a few minutes at the beginning or the end of the day to review—precisely!—your Community Building Efforts.

6. Reach out! Rolodex Communities must grow to be vital. Schedule at least one breakfast or lunch—per week—with someone new.

7. Prune! The "community" must be manageable. Don't be rude. Do be thoughtful about how you apportion your face time. (To repeat the obvious: *Time is Brand You's most finite/precious resource.*)

8. Consciously **n-u-r-t-u-r-e** your Rolodex Community. One of my tricks, inherited from my Stanford mentor Gene Webb, is my "Various Friends" correspondence. When I come across anything that turns me on, I consciously and immediately, while the spark still glows, distribute it to a select bunch of Members of My Community … with a brief cover note about why it tickled my fancy. Goal: Keep "them" … **consciously** … In The (My!) Loop.

9. *Think Rolodex.*

Think Community.

Constantly.

Brand You = Your Rolodex Is You.

22a.

LOYALTY. NEW LOYALTY.
NOT "LOGO LOYALTY."
BUT ROLODEX LOYALTY.
NETWORK LOYALTY.
COMMUNITY LOYALTY.
EXTENDED FAMILY LOYALTY.

The Nub

As an alumnus, I am not loyal to "McKinsey & Co." I am loyal—as Hell—to *My* McKinsey. That is, the individuals I loved/love and admired/admire ... and who are part of **My Rolodex Universe** ... 18 years after leaving "The Firm."

"Loyalty" is **not** on the decline, as so many would have it. At least that's my take. "Logo Loyalty"—to GE or GM or McKinsey—may well be on the decline. (*Great!* I never liked being an Indentured Servant ... or worshiping a Huge Institution.) But Rolodex/Network/Community Loyalty is on the rise. (If you are wise.) That is, in our context here, if you are a wise Brand You.

Hint: This is not news to the particle physicist. She may well be on the payroll of the University of Chicago. But her Community is ... unmistakably ... the Particle Physicists of the World, wherever they may happen to be. So, too, the English Department's Deconstructionists. (Or whatever.)

Why? Because these are the folks who aid, abet, and inspire you. These are the folks who are there when you have a problem ... and if they don't have the solution themselves, they'll search *their* Rolodexes to find someone who can help. They feed and nurture your curiosity, your conviction, your soul. These are the folks with whom you c-o-n-n-e-c-t.

The new loyalty is strong. *But* it's to Craft/Community ... not Logo. There is a difference. (A **b-i-g** difference.)

T.T.D./The New (But Profound) Loyalty

1. So are you care-ful (*full of care*) ... toward your Rolodex/Network/Community? Do you nurture them? (*Unfailingly?*) Come to their assistance? (*Unfailingly?*) Check on their well-being? (*Unfailingly?*) You're playing a New Game now: The Me Inc. Game (even if you decide ... for now ... to stay on someone's payroll). The Me Inc. "game" is the Ultimate Loyalty Game. Think about it. Act on it. Today. Every day. Consciously.

2. Define Rolodex Loyalty: What ... EXACTLY ... does it mean? As usual: Chat with a couple of colleagues. Talk about Loyalty. The New Loyalty: Rolodex Loyalty. How do you/we "operationalize" it? T-O-D-A-Y? On our ... Current Project? What should we add to our Daily Ritual ... in EXPLICIT SERVICE TO ROLODEX/EXTENDED FAMILY LOYALTY? List **t-e-n** "to-do" items.

23.

I think it was Warren Bennis who first talked to me about building a Personal University. And a McKinsey & Co. pal of mine, Allen Puckett, was the master. Allen would read a book, for example, then call the author and invite him to dinner the next time he was in the fellow's town. Over the years he "collected" a stunning array of Dazzling Resources that he called upon as needed.

The Nub

These are Freakish Times. No doubt of that. Hence: **You are as (appropriately) freakish as ... the Freaks You Collect.**

I don't know about you, but I obsess ... daily ... about what I **don't** know. What I'm **not** reading. Who I'm **not** hanging out with. Who **will** s-t-r-e-t-c-h me. Who **will** f-o-r-c-e me out of my Comfort Zone. Who **will** be so-damn-compelling that I'll be required to reexamine/toss out some basic tenets of my belief system.

I AM TERRIFIED OF ... STALE. Thence, I have but one choice: EXPOSE MYSELF—CONSTANTLY!—TO DE-STALERS. A.K.A.: FREAKS.

(Am I making [any] sense? To you? I pray that I am.)

So blasted easy to go to lunch with the Same Folks. **(Again.)** Read the Same Magazines. **(Again.)** Attend the Same Conferences. **(Again.)** Volunteer for jobs/projects where you "know what you're doing." **(Again.)** And so ... bloody ... hard ... to constantly expose yourself to contrarians ... contrarian ideas ... powerful enough to shake your faith ... in yourself.

But to restate the obvious (which needs restating, all the time): Hanging with the same folks, reading the same magazines, going to the same conferences is ... DEADLY. You simply cannot compete as Brand You if you're the same old same old.

IT IS DEAD, FLAT SIMPLE (to state). YOU'RE AS RICH-DIVERSE-FREAKY-COOL-"WITH IT" AS THE COOL/FREAKY/WITH-IT DUDES/DUDETTES YOU HANG WITH.

(It really is that ... simple. And that ... hard.)

T.T.D./The Take a Freak to Lunch Bunch!

1. You go to a cool restaurant. This Saturday. It rocks. On Monday, call the restaurateur. Invite her to lunch. Talk about stuff. Add her to your Cool Dudettes Collection.

2. Read a challenging article in *Wired* or *Business 2.0* or *Fast Company*. E-mail the author with your views. Start an e-spondence (e-correspondence). Invite him/her to dinner the next time your nonvirtual paths cross. Ask him/her what Cool/Weird Conferences he/she is going to. Pick one. Go to it.

3. Now. **RIGHT DAMN NOW.** Pick an oddball conference to go to … in the next 90 days. (Virtual World be damned. "Live conferencing" is more important than ever.) Go on your own nickel—spend the $2,000—if "the company" won't support it. Network Like Crazy!

4. Set up a Freak Collection section in your Rolodex. Add to it. Consciously. Constantly. Nurture it. Consciously. Constantly.

5. Repeat after me:

I AM AS COOL AS THE COOLNESS OF THE DUDES/DUDETTES I ASSOCIATE WITH.

24.

(And most of your competition … doesn't get it. At all.)

The Nub

DESIGN. This book is published by Alfred A. Knopf. The company made *I.D.*'s (*International Design* magazine.) Top 40 … the set of 40 most design-driven companies in America. (Disney and Bloomberg and Gillette and the New York Yankees were also on the list.) Design matters to publisher-guru Sonny Mehta at Knopf. A lot. The words (my words, in this case) count. But so does the presentation style thereof.

I've worked for five years—intimately—with my graphic design colleague, Ken Silvia. He is one of only five members of my Inner Group. The reason: **(1)** He's a Cool Dude. **(2)** He's awesome at what he does. **(3)** Design Matters. **(4)** A Lot. **(5)** To Me.

* **I THINK D-E-S-I-G-N.**

* I O-B-S-E-S-S DESIGN.

* I L-I-V-E DESIGN.

* D-A-I-L-Y.

And I urge you—in no uncertain terms—to do the same. **We—all!—"present ourselves" to numerous publics ... mostly "by design."** (Even if we are totally unaware/clueless. Which I was until recently.) We give off "design vibes" wherever we go: clothing, hairstyle, business cards, report style, presentation style, etc.

Since we give off these design clues/vibes whether we want to or not ... and since they are a major factor in the creation and success of Brand You ... shouldn't we try to control our design/beauty/destiny?

Another take: Designers' Laws are your Brand You "signage laws":

* Clarity!

* Economy!

* Excitement!

* Beauty!

* Grace!

* Friendliness!

* Integrity!

Problem: Most of us don't "think design." And that's what I want to change. Here. Now.

It's not that I think I can turn you into Picasso. (I can't.) (I have z-e-r-o artistic talent myself.)

But I do...arrogantly perhaps...think I can make you what I call Design Mindful. That is, I can urge/beg you to "be tuned into design." Be tuned into the fact that...

YOU—BRAND YOU!—PRESENT YOURSELF VIA "DESIGN CUES" EVERY MINUTE...OF EVERY DAY.

T.T.D./Design Obsession!

1. Don't do this alone. "It" needs a sounding board. With a trusted (sympathetic!) colleague: Begin the process of discussing/assessing how the two of you "present yourselves" to various publics...by design.

2. Stop. Make a list of **25** (no fewer!) design "items" that are a part of the Everyday-Presentation-of-You-to-Others. Assess—quantitatively?—each of the 25. (No kidding.)

3. Get two or three buddies together. **Invite a local designer to lunch or dinner.** Or ask—for a fee—her/him to "do" a half-day Design Consciousness Seminar for you and your gang in HR, IS, whatever.

4. Start to Open Your Eyes anew! Peruse some design mags. Look at Web sites through a Design Eye. (The Web is a pure design medium.) Record "Design Observations" in a notebook. (I've been doing this for eight years; it's simply a Consciousness-Raising "trick.")

25.

I have a "product line." As much as The Gap does. So do
you! I try constantly to add to mine: new areas of interest … new ways/styles/channels of communication …
new packaging … new value. You should consciously do
the same.

The Nub

My "staple" activity is 75 seminars a year. I punctuate
each one with 35mm slides. The 200+ slides I use on a
given day are the "currency" of my seminars. Moreover,
the 200+ slides are divided into about ten topic areas. I
am fanatical about this: I insist (to myself) that 25 percent (I measure meticulously) of the slides (slides =
ideas) be less than 90 days old. I want one of the ten
topic areas to be newly minted in the last six months.

(Nirvana: The salon owner who approached me after a
presentation to the Midwest Beauty Show in late February 1999 and said, gushing, "God, I went to one of your
seminars last year. Ninety percent of the stuff is new."
Well, that's not quite true … but I'm **delighted** she
perceives it that way.)

Bigger point(s):

* Brand Yous provide/"sell" products.

* The "products" are discrete (identifiable) "things."

* Taken together they represent—are!—a "product line." The **product line** must grow or else you … Brand You … are not growing. You are, in fact, declining. I.e.: It is grow … or decline. Period. Stasis is de facto decline.

* Think Product Line.

* Think Expansion thereof.

* Think c-o-n-s-c-i-o-u-s-l-y about this.

Recall that one of William Bridges's Eight Hats (item 9a) was the Product Development Hat. It's true! Product development! It is your/my business. Explicitly.

F-o-r-e-v-e-r.

T.T.D./Product Development at Me Inc.

1. Starting point: List your Current Product Portfolio. Do so in a … clear … succinct … market-oriented fashion. I.e.: What's the "specific stuff" I do that is worth paying good money for? (Review **The List** with close colleagues. Figuring out just what you do that's a "marketable product-service" is not as easy as it might seem at first blush.)

2. So ... where next? What **t-w-o** products do you plan to add to your Portfolio in the next six months? (BE SPECIFIC. NO FUDGING.)

3. Consciously set aside investment time. **Days** or **weeks** (not hours) when you work on "new stuff" to be added to your Product Portfolio.

YOU ARE ME INC. (At least in spirit.) **"GROWTH COMPANIES" INVEST—CONSCIOUSLY!—IN THE FUTURE. GREAT COMPANIES INVEST VIGOR-OUSLY/BOLDLY IN THE FUTURE. AND YOU?**

26.

The Nub

"You risk becoming a parody of yourself by not innovating," says sportscaster Keith Olbermann, "by saying, 'This works for me. Let me try to find a slight variation and make it look fresh.'"

I read those words in *Icon* a year or so ago. And I was moved—stunned!/scared shitless!—by them.

Olbermann is so right.

Line extensions (No. 25 above): We must always be adding to our "product" portfolio.

REMEMBER: THINK DISCRETE PRODUCT.

But we must also guard ... constantly ... as Brand You's ... against the "slight variations"/"parody of myself" trap that Olbermann brilliantly describes above.

Enter: The Big Idea.

> You can do homework from now until doomsday, but you will never win fame and fortune unless you also invent *big ideas.*
> —David Ogilvy

A **huge** idea, per ad genius Ogilvy again:

"Did it make me gasp when I first saw it?"

Gasp-worthiness doesn't happen every day (and it may never happen) ... but the quest in and of itself can lead to innovation/inspiration/aspiration.

T.T.D./ Parody Poison!

1. Talk with a Client: What should/could we be working on that's **Rad As Hell?** (Use those words ... or close equivalents. Okay?)

2. Have you got anything in your projected project portfolio that qualifies as a **_Makes Me Gasp_** idea? If not: Schedule—ASAP—some Dream Big Sessions (Gasp-ability Sessions?) with the Weirdest Cats you know. DREAM BIG. TALK BIG. THINK GASP. You'll doubtless not trip over the pot of gold at the end of the rainbow the first time out. But ... you've got to start somewhere!

3. Get comfortable with **Big, Gasp-worthy Ideas**. Think about ... and write down ... ten of what you consider Big Ideas. The space shuttle? Absolut ads? NATO? The euro? Twist-off bottle tops? Why are they Big Ideas? What do you suppose triggered them?

Start to think **B-I-G.**

27.

The Nub

The old economy says, Make a plan and stick to it. The new economy is so unformed, so out of the ballpark, that the rules are different: **Dream wild**, stick out your thumb, and climb aboard for the ride.... Be loose, be open to surprise, and be cool. —Harriet Rubin

Old White Collar World is crumbling. Fast. We will survive the turmoil to the extent that we stand for something ... big *and* bold *and* daring. Easy to write. (Very.) Hard to live. (Very.) The White Collar Professional ... per the (old-fashioned) Organization Man ... has not been asked to dare greatly for the last century and a half.

But...**now**...it's...stand up...stick your neck **way** out...and be counted...OR ELSE. (Be counted out.)

We've got to step out—painful or not—or else. (Or else: Be stepped on.) One more time: The Village Blacksmith—your great-great-great-grandfather—got this 200 or so years ago.

Now you and I have to "get it" *(g-l-o-r-i-o-u-s "it,"* as I see it): <u>WE ARE ON OUR OWN. IT'S UP TO US. TO MAKE OUR DARING MARK. OR ELSE.</u> (Redux.)

T.T.D./Step Way Out or ...
Step Way Down

1. Are you willing to: Risk Your (Professional) Life on Your Current Project? All I ask is: **THINK ABOUT IT.** Is the project cool enough/daring enough to be worthy of such risk?

2. Does my current project **"scare me shitless"**? That's how one WOW Project Maven put it ... about prospective Cool Stuff. Is it a bit (or more!) unnerving? If not, what ... specifically ... can I/we do about it? (Including: Stop doing what I'm doing ... even if it's politically awkward to do so.)

3. Personal prep: Add some derring-do outside of your work life. Sign up for a white-water rafting trip. Climb a mountain. **Try an Ethiopian restaurant.** Whatever. The idea: Get comfortable being uncomfortable.

28.

This is my life. I plan to make it count. I plan to make it memorable. I plan to give my all. I plan to … **make art** … in accounting … or information systems; in sales … or customer service.

I am Brand You. I am Performing Artist.

The Nub

Stanislavsky once wrote that you could play well or badly, but play truly. It is not up to you whether your performance will be brilliant—all that is under your control is your intention. It is not under your control whether your career will be brilliant—all that is under your control is your intention. If you intend to manipulate, to show, to impress, you may experience mild suffering and pleasant triumphs. If you intend to follow the truth you feel in yourself—to follow your common sense, and force your will to serve you in the quest for discipline and simplicity—you will subject yourself to profound despair, loneliness, and constant self-doubt. And if you persevere, the Theater, which you are learning to serve, will grace you, now and then, with the greatest exhilaration it is possible to know.

—David Mamet

Death is only one of many ways to lose your life.
> —Alvah Simon, *North to the Night,* the story of
> Simon's wintering over, alone, with his small
> boat locked in the polar ice

**The rewards and refreshments … come from the courage
to try something, all sorts of things, for the first time.
An enamored amateur need not be a genius to stay out
of ruts he has never been trained in. … Adventuring
amateurs reward us by a wonderful vagrancy into the
unexpected.**
> —Daniel Boorstin, historian

All the world's a stage: I l-o-v-e the Brand
You idea, the Brand You life. It is *my* life. *My* love. *My* art.
My craft. *My* performance. "They"—the suits—are simply my means for achieving distinction. (Not vice versa.)

Will I work hard? Much harder than when I was working
for "them." **I am.** I am Martha Stewart … in HR. (Why
not?) **I am.** I am Oprah in … Finance. (Why not?) The "Department" is my stage.

(I admit it. All this makes me tingle. My life.

My performance!

I can take it back from them. Oy vey … the joys of self-responsibility. Self-presentation.)

(You see … you'll never convince me that HR or IS is less
meaningful than The Stage. Don't even bother trying!)

I was in my hotel room following a **Performance**—an all-day seminar to top managers!—in Helsinki. BBC World Service aired a long interview with Rod Steiger. As he talked of his craft, of his rare moments of perfect theatrical pitch, I found myself tearing up. Maybe it was just the jet lag. But I don't think so.

I have been drawn more and more to reading and reportage about artists of all sorts … from Michael Jordan to Bob Dylan to Rod Steiger. I've had one or two of "those moments," when I achieved perfect pitch—complete concord—with my audience. And those moments draw me to the possibilities of all our work. Work that intends to matter!

"Performance" is a beautiful word, I think. I imagine Frank Gehry at work on the design of the Bilbao Guggenheim. Or one of IDEO Design & Product Development chief David Kelley's gang achieving perfect pitch while designing a medical instrument. Or my college mate, the renowned pediatric cardiologist Frank Galioto, **performing** an "impossible" surgical feat … and saving or extending a young life in the process.

Performances of consequence. In HR. Purchasing. IS. (God knows!) In short … I think they are within our grasp. But first, we must imagine:

Performances that Matter.

T.T.D./Performance!

1. Talk with a colleague or two, part or not part of your company, about ... Craft. About your Craft. Their Craft. I.e.:

Is a Day in the Projects ... a full-fledged Performance?

If not, is there something you can do ... **n-o-w** ... to enhance the excitement/theatricality of the current project ... to make it ... an act worthy of your wholesale commitment? Go slow on this. Start the dialogue with some friends. It is Your B-e-i-n-g, the Presentation of You, that is under discussion here.

* * *

Experiences are as distinct from services as services are from goods.
—Joseph Pine and James Gilmore, *The Experience Economy: Work Is Theater & Every Business a Stage*

* * *

2. Consider Daniel Boorstin's marvelous phrase "a wonderful vagrancy into the unexpected." What does that mean to you?

Have you taken any wonderful vagrancies recently?

Ever? What might lead you to take one? (Hint: Might Brand You be a wonderful vagrancy into the unexpected?)

29.

The Nub

Bosses: Please reread No. 28 above. Is it a threat? "They" aim to become "performing artists." With an Independent Streak a mile wide and a mile deep.

Doesn't that smack of disloyalty?

Y-E-S! P-R-A-I-S-E B-E! That is … it's the New Millennium. "We" will win—in this Age of Intellectual Capital— exactly to the degree that our "Talent" (née "workers") are proud, growing, Independent Actors … Determined to Make a Difference … Determined to **P**erform with Verve and Flair.

T-H-I-N-K A-B-O-U-T I-T.

T.T.D./ Bosses Rejoice! Loyalty Is Dead!

1. Bosses: Talk with your gang. About the changing world. The White Collar Revolution. Talk about Survival. Independence. Distinction. Performance. Initiate a Group Dialogue around Doing Cool Stuff. Around Accounting as Performing Art. Make this discussion the primary basis for concocting unit strategy!

2. Bosses: **WHAT HAVE YOU DONE—TODAY!— TO EXPLICITLY ENCOURAGE INDEPENDENT, RISK-SEEKING, PERFORMING ARTS, BRAND YOU—BUILDING BEHAVIOR WITH AT LEAST ONE KEY EMPLOYEE?**

(E.g.: Worked on reframing a project to ensure that it's a step way outside the normal bounds of departmental work? Encouraged someone to take a two-month sabbatical to learn some cool new skill?)

30.

Through single-minded devotion to the product, to the environment in which it appears and through the way in which it communicates, BMW has created a tangible image of itself. —Wally Olins, *Corporate Identity*

A distinguished, constantly-attended-to Identity is anyone's/any company's ... most cherished asset.

The Nub

If "identity" works for BMW ... it'll work for you ... if you work at it. Hard.

Olins redux: "Products from the major competing companies around the world will become increasingly similar. Inevitably, this means that the whole of the company's personality, its identity, will become the most significant factor in making a choice between one company and another."

All this sound a little grand for you/Brand-You-in-progress? I demur. I'm not (quite) urging you to become an egomaniac.

I am urging you to think—long and hard—about your I-D-E-N-T-I-T-Y. In BMW-ian terms.

Look to the arts. Fashion designers attempt to create identity far beyond the look of the season **(Calvin Klein, Giorgio Armani, Miuccia Prada.)** So, too, great movie actresses ... great chefs ... great architects.

All of my friends who are graphic designers or product designers—and most are not egomaniacs—think carefully about their appearance, their presentation style, their style in general. One great friend—a renowned graphic designer—will put as much character and personality into the presentation to two people in a barn, during a record-setting blizzard on Martha's Vineyard, as he does when he presents to Jan Wenner of *Rolling Stone* or Francis Ford Coppola. (I witnessed this with my own eyes in February 1999.)

That is, he doesn't turn his Identity on and off.

It is him.

And he gives his all ... all the time.

T.T.D./Identity!

1. **What does "Identity" mean?** It's a big deal! And if something is so big a deal, you should become a serious student. Right? Consider doing what I did. **Study.** For example, Wally Olins's *Corporate Identity.* Or Nicholas Kochan's *The World's Greatest Brands.* How about an Identity Study Group ... with a couple of friends in the same Brand-You-to-be boat?

2. List the Elements of Identity. **_(At least 15!)_** How do you do ... in terms of having carefully thought through these Attributes of Distinction?

3. Recruit a casual (or not-so-casual!) advisor ... from the Identity/Branding professional services. Invite her to address—and perhaps advise—your little band of concerned colleagues.

31.

My colleague Jim Kouzes and his partner Barry Posner have over a decade's worth of research that says **Credibility** is the/any leader's most prized resource. They've written a superb book with just that one word—Credibility—as its title. Ditto the story for Brand You.

The Nub

We talk—all too loosely—about a society becoming unhinged. I disagree. Totally. I have no affection for the old society where we were, per Dilbert, Cubicle Slaves. I like—love!—the New World Order, where we must be—once again!—In Charge of Our Own Lives. For good ... **or** for ill.

Thence, in the New Age of Self-Reliance, it becomes axiomatic: To operate effectively as Brand You we must be ... absolutely ... Trustworthy. And ... Credible.

Brand You's word is Brand You's bond! Brand You's credibility **is** the brand.

And I think: That's cool. **V-e-r-y** Cool.

I give seminars. All over the world. Johannesburg. Warsaw. Orlando. Auckland. Cincinnati. (I'm on my way to

Cincinnati as I write.) Snow. Ice. Hail. Tornadoes. No matter. Gotta show up. As scheduled. When scheduled. I must be … as a Brand You … absolutely … Trustworthy. Like Johnson & Johnson's Band-Aids. And Scotch tape. And Kleenex.

T-r-u-s-t-w-o-r-t-h-y. Worthy of Trust. <u>Arrive … on time. Come Hell **and** High Water. Deliver as promised.</u> (Or die trying.) (Almost literally.)

Brands = Cool. Sure! Brands = Trust. First and Foremost!

T.T.D./ Trustworthy (Worthy of Trust)

1. Ask yourself … mercilessly: Do I Exude Trust? **E-x-u-d-e.** Big Word. Do I "smack of" Trust? Think about it. Carefully.

2. I guess it sounds a little "spinnish," but "manage" trustworthiness. Explicitly. What have you done …

s-p-e-c-i-f-i-c-a-l-l-y

… in the last 24 hours to enhance your …

Image of …

TRUSTWORTHINESS?

3. I don't recommend a Trustworthiness Plan. (Too phony.) I do recommend that you do an informal daily-weekly "audit" of your actions:

Has my microbehavior (think through a half-dozen recent meetings) enhanced my Image of Trustworthiness? My Credibility? Explicitly?

And: Has anything I've done—especially some "small" thing—detracted from my Presentation of Trustworthiness & Credibility? Be specific. Be v-e-r-y hard on yourself.

4. T-E-L-L T-H-E T-R-U-T-H.

<u>Trustworthiness = Truthfulness</u>. I hope you won't feel I'm condescending to you with this obvious homily. Fact is, truth-telling is not all that common in Dilbert-ville. And conscientious corporate truth-tellers are a rather rare breed. Thence, <u>truthfulness is a "competitive advantage."</u> (Plus, you can look in the mirror without flinching.) For a "guide" on this topic, read Brad Blanton's *Radical Honesty*.

32.

(You heard it here first!) And often it starts with a Calling Card. Literally.

Calling cards, good or bad, tell a (surprisingly) Large Tale. Like the best packages, the best Calling Cards convey trustworthiness and WOW! at once. (We hope.)

The Nub

I have only 50 items to "spend." (Plus a little cheating … a few "22a's" etc.) So why in the world—in these chaotic times—would I devote an enormous, full 2 percent of my capital to the Calling Card?

Because … **FIRST THINGS FIRST.**

Calling Cards matter.

Calling Cards are your signature.

The first Sign of You is often your … Calling Card.

Calling Cards are … Cool.

Or … Not-So-Cool.

Calling Cards are ... *never* neutral.

I hired someone a couple of years ago because of ... her ... Calling Card. I exaggerate. I hired her because she was a Cool Dudette. But my first strong tip-off was her Calling Card ... which stood **w-a-y out** amidst a stack of well over 200 résumés. It was exactly enough to make me ... instantly ... put her résumé into the "Second Look Pile."

(B-I-G Deal!)

It is exactly as important to you (and me) as it is to BMW or Nike or Apple. Maybe more important (maybe far more important): It is one of the few ways you can ... initially and instantly ... stand (way) apart from the Herd.

TOM PETERS
CHAIRMAN

EMAIL tom@tompeters.com

WEB www.tompeters.com

tompeters! compan

T.T.D./A Calling Card Obsession!

1. Reread the above. Off (on your own) or (still) on someone's payroll ... O-B-S-E-S-S on your Calling Card.

2. Study—yes!—Calling Cards. (Start by reading this book: *What Your Business Card Reveals About You—and How to Fix It*, by Lynella Grant.)

3. Can you say ... **confidently** ... that your Calling Card/Letterhead is **The Signature** you want of you/Brand You? (Think—hard!—before you answer. PLEASE.)

4. Spend $$$ on this. Few Brand You "investments" are more important than Calling Cards/Letterhead.

5. *Does your "mere" Calling Card reflect ... exactly ... Who You Are? Exactly ... How You Are Special?* **(Are you sure?)**

33.

Short message: If you don't have a Web site ... get one. It need not be fancy. But it can be of extraordinary value (e.g.: community-building, identity-creating, Client-attracting); and it signals that you're "with the program" (not stuck in the Dark Ages). Or at least not "not with the program."

The Nub

Brand You: The Web is your Friend. Perhaps your Best Friend. The Web is the great equalizer. Levels the playing field. It lets cool/small outpace dull/big.

There's an excitement to the Web that's palpable. It is changing the way we live ... in a million ways ... forever. Don't deprive yourself of this epoch-making tool.

At its best, the Web allows **Playful, Distinct You to Do Something R-e-a-l-l-y Cool**. To provide info and ideas in a friendly/exciting format. For instance: Create community chat groups around Ideas You Care About. That's one ticket for the determined Web-ist. (Bless you. Smart you.)

For the more tentative, at least the Web can be a solid, professional Place Mark. <u>You can keep a little info about you "on file for the world." Demonstrate that you are in the game.</u>

You *must* do ... **s-o-m-e-t-h-i-n-g**. But I don't advise you to go for it big ... unless you really are tuned in and turned on. (Why? Because it's absorbing work ... and your energies may be more productively spent elsewhere. Which doesn't mean you can't hire a part-time Web-fanatic to handle this aspect of Brand You.)

Above all ... don't get cute. Unsexy Web sites trying to be Sexy are a pretty sorry sight. (The sorriest of sites.)

ICON WOMAN MEETS THE WEB

It *is* a Web World! Remember Icon Woman? (See No. 4a.) She is also Web Woman. I.e.: She ...

* submits her résumé for a new job on the Web.

* is recruited on the Web.

* negotiates via e-mail.

* is hired on the Web.

* is trained on the Web.

* creates and conducts projects on the Web.

* manages project and Client follow-up on the Web.

* manages her career and reputation-building (Brand You development!) on the Web.

I.e.: "It" is becoming the whole Enchilada.

T.T.D./ Web World and Brand You— Web World *Is* Brand You

1. For starters: Spend time on the Web. **Every Day.** Get comfortable with it. Use it. Assess sites. What works? What doesn't? What's a turn-on? What's a turnoff? Look at the Big Picture. At the minutiae.

2. At least consider—damn seriously—a Bare Bones Site with information about you. It's not just a start. It's a good start. So … Do It. **(Now.) (Even if** you are still on someone's payroll.) (Starting per se is *the* ticket!)

3. *If you are at all inclined, consider the Bold Option. (The Web is made for you!) What if Your Site were a Cool Place … where Cool Folks … talk about Cool Stuff? THIS IS NOT— AT ALL!—BEYOND THE IMAGINABLE. If you're in a playful mood, find a super-Web-savvy buddy or two … and consider … Going For It. (Money ain't the issue. Commitment/Time is.)*

4. Grander yet:

Consider a Web Strategy for Branding Yourself … and Selling Your Services.

This, again, is no great stretch in the New Millennium world. The great news: You can "meet" pals/experts on line who will help you with this. (IT IS SWEET.)

34.

Building a local reputation is part and parcel of building Brand You. That means using most any opportunity to ... **Tell Your Story.** Part of that means skills at orally communicating with at least a few others. You don't need to aim for JFK's league, but you do need to have "public speaking" in your repertoire, which is why I so wholeheartedly recommend Toastmasters.

The Nub

You don't have to be Ronald Wilson Reagan. Or John Fitzgerald Kennedy.

But Brand You World ... is ... Sales World.

That is, Presentation-of-You is important. (Very.)

One (b-i-g) idea. Tame your (v-e-r-y natural!) fear of public speaking. There are doubtless lots of strategies for this. I am an unabashed Toastmasters fan. Toastmasters is a bit too structured for me, but that's the smallest annoyance. It is a premier self-help organization that has led hundreds of thousands to master Self-Presentation.

I have no association with Toastmasters. At all. And there are several alternatives. That's not my point. My point is: You do not have to become the Great Communicator. **But it would be dishonest to suggest that the new Brand You world doesn't demand more attention than in the past to Self-Presentation skills.** (I.e.: Being very good at this is worth its weight in more than mere gold.)

TOM'S "RULES FOR GETTIN' GOOD AT SPEECHIFYING"

1. Join Toastmasters.

2. *See No. 1 above.*

3. Practice.

4. **Practice.** Find any excuse to say a few Public Words at a community meeting, etc.

5. Use volunteer work as a (the!) training ground ... fund-raising ... religious organization officer ... PTA officer.

6. It's normal to be nervous. *I still am.*

7. Don't open your mouth (in public) unless you are Passionate about your Point of View. Passion-Credibility-Care is what you "sell" as a Speaker-Communicator. Regardless of subject.

8. Focus.

9. Focus.

10. Focus. Use 5 x 7-inch—or better yet, 3 x 5-inch notecards with Key Points. Polish the Hell out of these Key Points. Limit them to five ... or fewer.

11. Practice. On your spouse. Significant other. Best pal. Kids. Cabdriver. Your Australian shepherd.

12. Don't memorize. Don't read. Stiff Kills.

13. *Don't tell jokes.*

14. Be timely. Tie your remarks to some event reported in today's newspaper.

15. If you use audiovisual aids ... keep 'em clear and simple. Exploiting PowerPoint's full potential with sexy, multicolored graphs and charts is ... disastrous. (Trust me.)

16. **Repeat yourself.** Keep your basic ideas down to four or five ... and hammer them home in ten different ways each.

17. Tell stories! **Great Speechifying = Great Storytelling.** Period.

18. Notice how presidents of the United States bring living examples—heroes like Rosa Parks and Sammy Sosa—to State of the Union speeches. Is there anyone in your audience you could salute? And whose story dramatizes your point?

19. Make (all) your stories "human interest" stories. Real People (in the company, customers, vendors) doing Real Stuff.

20. Use simple, compelling handouts that summarize your key points.

21. Try not to be defensive. (Much easier said than done!) You are here to Win Friends and Influence People ... not make enemies or show off your superior intellect.

22. Never, ever, ever, ever, talk down to your audience. Show t-o-t-a-l respect. They deserve it! (Whoever they are.)

23. Solve your audience members' problems. Your proposal-plea should have something in it for them … personally. Great fund-raisers say that they are "helping donors make cool investments in the future that they'll feel good about."

24. Make eye contact. (Easier said than done.) *You connect with only one person at a time.* (Even, for me, in an audience of thousands.) You speak to only o-n-e other fellow human being.

25. Seek out—with your eyes—your supporters. They already love you. And their positive body language will calm you down. (Trust me. This ain't no small thing.)

26. Ignore most rigid speaking rules. You don't need a peppy start to "grab" your audience. Nor a sexy finish. You need four or five clear points … to which you are **Totally Committed** … which you somehow, by hook and by crook, convey in your 10 or 50 minutes.

27. You will … somehow … get another chance. So don't put yourself under the now-or-never gun. It's 94 percent false.

28. <u>Be modest and self-deprecating.</u> Nothing is a bigger turnoff than arrogance or boasting. (Al Gore is still trying to live down his claim to have invented the Internet. It may cost him the presidency.)

T.T.D. / Self-Presentation Excellence ... or Else!

1. First, a little honest Self-Assessment. **How are your presentation skills? Be gentle ... but honest.**

2. If the answer is "in need of Help" ... which it is for 95 percent of us (99 percent?) ... then start thinking about what you can do ... STARTING NOW ... to work on this Big Brand You Issue (opportunity!).

3. Consider Toastmasters. Or some other formal "course work." (This isn't a casual deal. It's your life that's at stake. No?)

4. This is worth time-consuming consideration. This is no joke in Brand You World. <u>Self-presentation is a staple worthy of extreme, obsessive s-t-u-d-y. Brand You = A Performance. Brand You = A Distinct Entity.</u> I am not trying to make you what you are not. I am begging you to believe you can get much better at the Self-Presentation of You. Accept Student-hood ... just as the judo novice would. Self-presentation is an Honorable Task ... worthy of your intense scrutiny and application.

5. Invite an actor or actress from the local theater company to a Brown Bag Lunch Session with you and your colleagues. Have him or her chat with you about the Art of Self-Presentation ... and how you can get better at it with application.

35.

The Nub

I am a shameless dispenser of enthusiasm.
—Benjamin Zander, conductor, Boston Philharmonic

If you're bumming out, you're not going to make it
to the top. [So ...] we might as well make a point of
grooving.
—Scott Fischer, prior to an assault on Mount Everest

Okay, you're not the life of the party. No problem. (*I'm
not either. Understatement.*)

But you would do well to follow Tony Robbins's advice
and practice your smile before a mirror. (The Buddhists
said this long before Robbins. Smiling—per se—relaxes
you.) It's a fact: Upbeat wins. Inspires others. (Or ... smiles
beget smiles ... whatever.)

This is tough as Hell for me to talk about. And damn
personal. I am a pretty gloomy guy. Prozac user. (Not to
heighten performance ... but to dispel a little of the
semipermanent pall.)

So I'm never going to tell you to Smile and Be Happy. N-e-v-e-r.

I will tell you what I have learned: <u>That those who exude optimism and self-confidence inspire optimism and self-confidence in others.</u>

No miracles asked for here. (Can't do 'em for myself.) But I have learned to Pump Myself. Regularly....

<u>To practice a Smile before the mirror.</u> To put on a Clean Shirt before the afternoon half of my presentation.

Makes me feel fresh. (Big difference.) To do my daily Aerobic Exercise. (My current streak is at 278 days, as I write this.) To get out in the sun—or at least outside—in the early morning when I'm on the road. Even if it's only for 10 minutes. (Or 5.) To take stretch breaks of 15 minutes—or at least 3 minutes!—during the day. To practice very simple meditative breathing exercises.

This is not the Course in Miracles. It is to say that <u>Brand Yous up the odds of success with a positive mental attitude, to use the hopelessly hackneyed term. It *is* worth working on. And it *can* be worked on.</u> I **work** on it. And it helps. (Look we all have demons, baggage, anxieties ... the trick is in controlling them. And <u>we all have optimism, gifts, spirit ... the trick is in tapping into them.</u>)

T.T.D./Practiced Optimism

1. (Successful) Brand Yous smile a lot. **_Okay?_** (Successful) Brand Yous laugh a lot. **_Okay?_** So treat "it"... Practiced Optimism...as a Core Competence. Why? **It is!**

2. Do a little—or a lot, it's a big deal—of "self-help stuff" here. Read a bunch of stuff. Take a simple meditation course, perhaps. Treat this as a "problem"/"opportunity" to be "examined"/"worked at." It is. It can be. <u>Find out what makes you feel good</u>—a brisk walk, a phone call to a widowed aunt, mega-vitamins, a ten-minute chair massage, walking around barefoot for five minutes—<u>and practice it. Regularly</u>. Remember: What works for some doesn't for others. The key is to find what nurtures your spirit/soul/outlook.

3. As usual: Work with some intimate pals on this. Form a **_Grinners Anonymous Support Group._** Or even ... dare I say it ... consider a shrink (if you are a naturally gloomy sort). Working hard at Self-Worth is a WOW! Project of the First Order.

36.

I'm someone who's always tried systematically to destroy the very basis of my record-buying public. That's what keeps me alive. You destroy what you did before and you're free to carry on.
—Neil Young

The Nub

RENEWAL.

JOB 1.

PERIOD.

Great companies—from 3M to P&G—live off R&D. You are now Me Inc./Brand You. Aiming to be a Great Company in your own individual right. So ... think 3M. Think P&G. Think Research and Development. Or ... Renewal. Obsess on it. Do something about it.

E-v-e-r-y d-a-y.

It's an irony. Or paradox. The times beg us to run around like the proverbial chicken with its head cut off. And they simultaneously demand creativity, which usually comes from reflection and a commitment to "offline" growth.

Go figure.

Or: Do both. (I hate such mealy-mouthed advice. But it's justified here. The only trick is figuring out the trick.)

The good news: If you have the Personal R&D/Renewal Mindset, you can turn the hurly-burly of daily affairs into de facto R&D. Consummate Brand You and purposeful job jumper Veronique Vienne, who plies her trade in the fashion industry, summarizes brilliantly: *"My only single 'career strategy' is to plan what I can learn from each job."*

Every assignment—grand or tiny—should broaden you. Or else. Or else: Reject it! Ditto personal experiences outside your professional life. GROWTH IS ME. PERIOD.

THE SPIRIT OF RENEWAL

The following ... from an article in *Glamour* (September 1998). I.e.: Why renewal?

* "To cultivate openness."/"The mind of the beginner is ... open to all the possibilities."

* "To make a better living."/"Education equals earning power."

* "To discover your hidden passions."/"She ended up getting a second ... degree in horticulture and changing careers."

* "To grow a crop of hope."/"Remember how you learned to snowboard last winter? ... You started shaky and despairing but soon gained confidence."

* "To build a better brain."/**Tackling a novel task ... actually creates new nerve synapses and blood vessels in the brain.**

* "To improve your problem-solving and decision-making skills."

* "To meet new people."

* "To banish the blues."/Merlin to Arthur, per T. H. White in *The Once and Future King*: "The best thing for being sad is to learn something. That is the only thing that never fails, the only thing the mind can never exhaust, never alienate, never be tortured by, never fear or distrust and never dream of regretting."

* "Because life is a series of refresher courses."

* "Because learning something new is so damn much fun."

T.T.D./ Renewal-Personal R&D as Job No. 1

1. So what ... *specifically* ... have you learned in the last week? (Please try to answer this question. Precisely. Please repeat. Weekly.)

2. Does your current project have explicit (to you/for you) ... Learning Goals? At least two or three. Again: E-x-p-l-i-c-i-t. If not... RESTRUCTURE IT... now... even at the 75 percent point... to stretch yourself. Measurably.

3. Make this a... **Team Sport.** Meet (informally?) with your colleagues around the idea of: What have we learned that's new/Cool from this project? *(In the last 10 days?)* How can we reframe the project to serve our collective Learning Goals? *(Precisely?)*

4. How about a Renewal Buddy? (Spouse is fine.) Work with him/her on a pretty explicit Growth/ Learning Plan. (Hey, pharmaceutical companies live... or die... from massive injections of R&D. Obviously. You, too. Less obviously. Just as surely.)

5. How about a big version of No. 4 above... a Renewal Club? Say, ten of you. From different companies, who make a ... **Personal Growth Pact** ... and meet monthly, with outside speakers invited, to work on stretch. (Think of it as Planned Mental Aerobics.)

37.

Staying personally/professionally fresh demands a refreshment-investment plan as much as financial security demands a formal investment plan. (Career security = Renewal Investment. High security = High Investment.) Attributes of a Renewal Investment Plan.

* Formal

* Written

* Updated quarterly

* Reviewed by yourself weekly

* Reviewed with key advisors/trusted colleagues from time to time

* New skills (stretch!)

* New people (contacts! freaks!)

* New projects (stretch!)

* New off-the-job stuff (stretch!)

* At least one new thing to add to your résumé (quarterly)

The underlying message here: The onus for formal ("personnel") evaluation has passed ... from the organization ... to the individual.

You are your own judge.

Period.

Awesome responsibility. Awesome opportunity.

The Nub

FORMAL.

RENEWAL INVESTMENT PLAN.

P-E-R-I-O-D.

We are all—me, surely!—**R.D.A.s**, or Rapidly Depreciating Assets. "Cute phrase, Tom," you say. (At best.) "Dead serious," I rejoin.

Depreciation in the old (physical ... remember?) world of Chemical Plants is answered with Aggressive Investment.

Aggressive Investment starts with a ... plan. Or for me, relative to me: a Renewal Investment Plan. (Some suggestive attributes of which are listed above.)

Bottom, no-bull line: There is no excuse for not having a formal, aggressive R.I.P. (Can you think of any?)

1. **Brand Yous Renew.**

Obsessively.

Agressively.

Formally.

So today ... this week ... start the formal outline of your ... **Renewal Investment Plan.**

2. Hustle. (It's important.) Take your time. (It's serious.) That is ... get to work, but t-h-i-n-k. A Renewal Investment Plan is not something you dash off in an hour.

3. As usual (in this book ... and in this series), it'll work better as a Team Activity. (THE GREAT PARADOX: WE ARE TALKING ABOUT HEIGHTENED INDIVIDUALISM—BRAND YOU—WHICH DEMANDS HEIGHTENED COMMUNITY TO SUPPORT SUCH A VENTURE-ADVENTURE.) "Work it" (R.I.P.) with work colleagues. Or a set of empathetic pals.

4. Does your Renewal Investment Plan reflect each of the categories above (new skills, new people, new projects, exciting new off-the-job stuff)?

5. Invite a Capital Projects Planner to speak to you and your colleagues. Or a personal financial planner. Topic: the elements of planning for a future where ...

Growth = Safety.

38.

The most important thing about education is appetite.
—Winston Churchill

He is fundamentally about self-improvement. [He's a] learning machine.
—Mike McCue, Tell Me Networks, on Marc Andreessen, creator of the Web search engine and AOL Chief Technology Officer

My favorite people (Brand Yous) are ... CURIOSITY FREAKS. They are voracious ... insatiable ... relentless. They learn from anyone and any situation. Catholic tastes are a (big) part of Brand You success. E.g.: The great professional service practitioners bring an extra-ordinary breadth of experience to bear on any given project.

To Succeed: **Me Inc. = Curiosity Inc.**

The Nub

Big League Renewal = Planned, Passionate Curiosity.

A 50LIST WITHIN A 50LIST:
THE RENEWAL50

Renewal=

1. *Go to the nearest magazine shop.* Now. Spend 20 minutes. Pick up 20—**twenty!**—magazines. None should be ones you normally read. Spend the better part of a day perusing them. Tear stuff out. Make notes. Create files. Goal: Stretch! Repeat...monthly...or at least bimonthly.

2. *Go to the Web.* Now. Relax. Follow your bliss! Visit at least **15** sites you haven't visited before. Follow any chain that is even a little intriguing. Bookmark a few of the best. Repeat...at least once a week.

3. *Take off this Wednesday afternoon.* Wander the closest mall...for two hours. Note the stuff you like. (And hate.) Products, merchandising, whatever. Repeat ... bimonthly.

4. *Buy a packet of 3 x 5-inch notecards.* Carry them around with you. Always. Record cool stuff. Awful stuff. Daily. Review your card pack every Sunday. *(Obsess on this!)*

5. *Going the same place for vacation next year?* Why not someplace new? Why not one of those university-sponsored 12-day trips to explore some weird phenomenon?

6. *Project stuck in a rut?* Look through your Rolodex. Who's the oddest duck in there? Call her/him. Invite her/him to lunch. Pick her/his brain for a couple of hours about your project.

7. ***Create a new habit: Visit your Rolodex.*** Once a month. Pick a name of someone interesting you've lost touch with. Take her/him to lunch ... next week.

8. ***New habit: You're in a meeting.*** Someone you don't know makes an interesting contribution. Invite him/her to lunch ... in the next two weeks.

9. ***You run across somebody interesting.*** As a matter of course, ask her (him) what's the best thing she/he's read in the last 90 days. Order it from Amazon.com ... this afternoon.

10. ***Take tomorrow afternoon off.*** Rain or shine. Wander a corner of the city you've never explored before.

11. ***Go to the local Rite Aid.*** Buy a $2 notebook. Title it *Observations I*. Start recording. Now. Anything and everything. (Now = **Now.**)

12. ***Going out this Saturday night?*** Go some place new.

13. ***Having a dinner party next Sunday?*** Invite somebody—**interesting**—you've never invited before. (Odds are, he/she won't accept. So what? Go for it. It's just like selling encyclopedias. No ring doorbell = No sale.)

14. ***Go past a kiosk advertising local Community College courses for this fall.*** (Or one of the Learning Annex catalogues.) Grab a copy. Look it over this evening. Pick a couple of interesting courses and topics you've always wanted to know more about. Call the professor (with a little detective work, you can find her). If you're intrigued, sign up and ... at least ... go to the orientation session.

15. *Read a provocative article in a business journal.* Triggers a thought? E-mail the author. So what if you never hear back? (The odds are actually pretty high that you will. Trust me.)

16. *At church this Sunday, the pastor announces a new fund drive.* Sure you're busy. (Who isn't?) Go to the organizing meeting after services. Sign up!

17. *You're working with your 13-year-old on his science project.* You find you're having fun. Go to school with him tomorrow... and volunteer to talk to the class about the topic.

18. *A crummy little assignment comes along.* But it would give you a chance to work with a group of people you've never worked with before. Take the assignment.

19. *You're really pissed off at what's going on in your kid's school.* So run for the school board.

20. *You aren't really interested in changing jobs.* But there's a neat job fair in the next town this weekend. Go.

21. *An old college pal of yours invites you to go on a long weekend by the lake.* You never do things like that. Go.

22. *A really cool job opening overseas comes up.* It fits your skill set. You couldn't possibly consider it. You've got a nine-year-old and your husband is content with his job. At least call someone... and find out more about it.

23. *You're on the fast track.* But a fascinating job opens up... far away. It looks like a detour. But you could learn something really new. Really cool. Go talk to the guy/gal about it. (Now.)

24. *The eighth grade teacher is looking for chaperones for the trip to the natural history museum.* You're a law firm partner, for God's sake, making $350,000 a year. Volunteer.

25. *You love taking pictures.* You pick up a brochure advertising a four-day photography workshop in Maine next summer. Go to the workshop.

26. *A friend of yours, a small-business owner, is going to Thailand on a sourcing trip.* She invites you to join her. Go.

27. *There's a great ball game on ESPN in an hour.* Forget it. Go on that walk you love ... that you haven't taken for a year.

28. *I'm not much on planning.* But how about sitting down with your spouse/significant other and making a list of three or four things you've "been meaning to do" that are novel ... then coming up with a scheme for doing at least one of them in the next nine months?

29. *You've a-l-w-a-y-s wanted to go to the Yucatan.* So at least call a travel agent ... this week. *(How about right now?)*

30. *You know "the action is at the front line."* Spend a month (two days a week) on a self-styled training program that rotates you through all the front-line jobs in the hotel/distribution center/whatever.

31. *Ask a first-line supervisor who the most motivated clerk in the store is.* Take him/her to lunch ... in the next three weeks.

32. *You spot a Cool Article in the division newsletter.* Call the person involved. Take her/him to lunch. Tomorrow. Learn more. (Repeat.) (Regularly.)

33. *You and your spouse go to a great play this Saturday.* On Monday, call the director and ask him/her if you can come by and chat some time in the next two weeks. (If the chat goes well, ask her/him to come in to address your 18 colleagues in the Accounting Dept. at a Brown Bag Lunch Session later this month.)

34. *Institute a monthly Brown Bag Lunch Session.* Encourage all your colleagues to nominate interesting people to be invited. Criterion: "I wouldn't have expected us to invite ———."

35. *Volunteer to take charge of recruiting for the next year/six months.* Seek out input/applications from places the unit has never approached before.

36. *Consider a ... four-month sabbatical.*

37. *Get up from your desk.* Now. Take a two-hour walk on the beach. In the hills. Whatever. Repeat ... once every couple of weeks. (Weekly?)

38. *Seriously consider approaching your boss about working a day a week at home.*

39. *Take the door off your office.*

40. *You've got a couple of pals who are readers.* Start a Reading Group that gets together every third Thursday. Include stuff that's pretty far out. (Invite a noteworthy local author to talk to your group now and again.)

41. *Join Toastmasters.* (I know it's a repeat. It's important!)

42. *Pen an article for the division newsletter.*

43. *In the quarterly alumni magazine, you read about a pal who's chosen to do something offbeat with her life.* Call her. Tomorrow. (Or today.)

44. *Buy that surprisingly colorful outfit you saw yesterday.* Wear it to work. Tomorrow.

45. *Develop a set of probing questions to use at meetings.* "Will this really make a difference?" "Will anybody remember what we're doing here two years from now?" "Can we brag to our spouse/kids about this project?"

46. *Assess every project you propose by the "WOW!"/ "Is it Worth Doing?" criteria.*

47. *Call the Principal Client for your last project.* Ask her to lunch. Within the next two weeks. Conduct a no-holds-barred debriefing on how you and your team did ... and might have done.

Now.

48. *Call the wisest person you know.* (A fabulous professor you had 15 years ago?) Ask her/him to lunch. Ask her/him if he or she would be willing to sit with you for a couple of hours every quarter to talk about what you've done/where you're going. (Try it. It can't hurt.)

49. *Become a Cub Scout/Brownie troop leader.* Or direct your kid's play at school. The idea: spend more time

around children ... they're fascinating ... spontaneous ... and wise.

50. *Build a great sandcastle!*

T.T.D./Get Goin' Around Renewal!

1. See the 50List within a 50List above. **Pick 10.** Now. Get going.

2. Do it (redux) as a Team Sport ... with Colleagues/ Pals/Workmates who ... "Get It."

38a.

LOVE THE PLATEAU.

The Nub

George Leonard's marvelous book *Mastery* is a rare treatise on "getting good at something." There's a lot in it I love. (All of it, actually.) But one thing in particular: learning to love the plateau.

Leonard makes it clear—few others do—that "learning" and "mastery" are not a smooth ride up a neat slope, with a steady gradient. (No matter how hard you work.) You accomplish something: you launch a scintillating training program. And then you get stuck. (Badly.) Or even regress. Per Leonard: normal as Hell! We get "better" at any thing ... in a predictable way. We work like the blazes.

We have a good—Breakthrough!—day. (Or perhaps two.) Then we slip. And "stall" on a Plateau, as the lessons subconsciously sink in. Could last months. (Or years.) And then we "get it" ... and it becomes instinctive. And then eventually ... if we work like the blazes (redux) ... we have another Leap.

The point: Most of Life is spent on that Plateau. It may (does!) feel dreary at times. But it is the essence of (long-term) performance enhancement/mastery.

So: Since the plateau is the norm, Leonard counsels, learn to cherish it ... rather than fight it.

I.e., don't beat yourself up if you're having a slow day (week, month); know that all sorts of worthwhile things are happening beneath the surface. You're absorbing what you've learned. Your mind and body are integrating new information/responses/skills into its circuitry. Be gentle on yourself when you're plateauing. (*Caveat*: This is not to be interpreted as a license to waste time.)

The Big Idea:

We—Brand Yous—are necessarily on a long, often painful Journey to (we hope!) Mastery.

It's worth the Candle. (For Brand Yous, there is no other worthy Candle!) It's spotty, sporadic, marked by more downs than ups. But it is … clearly … the only path … if we want our Work to Matter.

T.T.D./ Plateau Passion!

1. Become a serious student of the Learning/Growth/Mastery Process! (Not many are. That must change if we want the process of approaching Mastery to become the norm. Which it must be for … Brand You.) Start by reading/inhaling George Leonard's *Mastery.* (It changed my life.)

2. Meet with stellar local professionals—chefs, architects, professors, surgeons. Talk with them about their Journey to Mastery. Learn, if you can, from their experiences. Become a dispassionate observer of your own learning path … and use your new self-knowledge about growth to guide, among other things, your selection of projects and your renewal goals.

39.

Me Inc. and Brand You (even if you're still on someone's payroll) = You're on your own. At least psychologically. Great! And not so great. Brand Yous need trustworthy pals. But I'm urging more here: an informal—or semi-formal—Board of Directors. That is, two or three or four or five people you respect, with whom you can sit down every quarter to review—rather formally—your progress and plans and stumbles. And to whom you can turn when your Exciting Project gets you in scalding water with The Suits. (It will if it's worthwhile.)

The Nub

Any Venture Worth Doing is a Pirate Venture. (At least at first.) That's a no-brainer. Which means it's … in the Establishment's face. So fight Establishment … with … Establishment.

Garner your own Advisory Board/Board of Directors. Respectable Closet Renegades … who support your in-surgency. **IN SHORT: YOU NEED COVER … IF YOU ARE DOING SERIOUSLY C-O-O-L STUFF.**

I've done one hyper-"cool" project in a big joint … McKinsey & Co. (Home to ultra-conservatism.) No doubt: The ability to move forward—far beyond the respectable bounds—was due to my cover, the Closet Renegades who came to our meetings, gave us Early Respectability.

Message:

All Revolutionaries need Respectable Cover. And the Wisdom of Trusted Elders.

So contact, cultivate, nurture like-minded souls who are higher up the food chain than you are. They will require care and feeding, but it's worth the effort. (Hint: appeal to their altruism ... *and* their self-interest.)

T.T.D./"Official" Advisors = A Must

1. You're on a Mission. Brand You's Mission to Cool. Trust me: You **n-e-e-d** a "respectable" cover ... a.k.a. Advisory Board/Board of Directors. (At least, informal.) So: **(1)** Face it. **(2)** Find them. **(3)** Cultivate them. **(4)** Use them. **(5)** Encourage them to use you.

2. Good News: In my experience the Establishment always includes a few Closet Renegades. They need you as much as you need them! They admire your spunk. And through you, they get to relive their Pirate Youth. *And:* They get their current kicks out of mentoring Junior Pirates. So: Recruit them! Shamelessly! I.e.: Start today. Schedule a couple of breakfasts or lunches in the next two weeks with, say, former bosses who took a shine to your aggressive approach to life.

3. Once "the board" is on board, schedule regular meetings with each member. Go out of your way keep each one in the loop. And: Don't be afraid to seek their counsel when you're in a tough or embarrassing corner— that's the point of the exercise!

40.

Great consultants make a beeline for the Front Line
... to get the Straight Scoop on any damn thing. Any
problem. Any process. **Make their habit your habit.**
Nurture a rich cadre of Front Line Folks with whom you
can test the pulse of the organization ... and the results
of your work.

The Nub

**All bosses are a-l-w-a-y-s out of
touch.** The best of them. That's Great News for Brand
You. (And for ... me. To this day.)

The analyst/problem solver who is nothing short of
determined to be in constant, direct touch with the
Front Line Folks always—**!!!**—has Ten Full Steps on "the
competition."

To this day, it remains the best-kept secret in the
business (why? beats me): She/he who is best in touch
with Real People Who Do the Work ... wins. Almost
unfailingly.

It's not that "they" (at the "front") are uniquely
smart. (Although they are "uniquely" in touch.) Or that

managers are particularly "dumb." (Though they are particularly "out-of-touch.") It's just that "their" (front-liners) info is by definition unfiltered … fresh … real. (We all know what happens to information as it moves up the organizational food chain. Even in the "best" places, it gets watered down and/or tarted up to make those passing it along look better. And even if intent is pure, it still becomes hopelessly distorted through repetition.)

As I see it:

Brand You Nirvana = Unfiltered Info

For me, this is a 33-year-old habit … instilled in me as a young Navy officer in Vietnam in 1966: The real info resides on the firing line. Biased information? Yes! (We all have biases!) But … go there. Repeatedly. Absorb. Reflect. Use. (Period.)

I'VE NEVER FORGOTTEN. At the highfalutin' McKinsey & Co. my best mentors retaught me The Lesson: that the "wizened old fellow with the green eyeshades" who lives Closest to the Problem/Issue/Action has the Clearest Take on it. (Duh.) (But, again, if "duh," then why do so few religiously practice the beeline-for-the-front-line style?)

Nascent Brand Yous:

Head for the Front Line.

Listen. **L-I-S-T-E-N.** Learn. **L-E-A-R-N.** Make contacts. Create no less than a Front Line University. And prosper accordingly. It truly is ... that simple.

(**Cool benefit.**: You meet neat people ... who deeply appreciate your interest. And c-a-r-e. Who have been waiting for the likes of you—a Listener—for **25 years**. Sometimes ... literally.)

T.T.D./Front Line University, Recruitment of

1. Regarding your Current Project: Have you Hung Out With/*Lived With* the Front Liners affected by it? *(Don't bullshit yourself about this.)*

2. Look at next week's calendar. Is extensive Front Line contact/observation part of it? (Redux: *Don't bullshit yourself about this.)*

3. Do you have no-baloney, formal Front Line Advisors on your Core Project Team? (If not, why not? If not, what do you plan to do about it ... **now**?)

4. Have you trained—i.e., browbeaten—all your teammates about Front Line Intimacy? (Again ... and again ... and again.)

5. Is this (Front Line Intimacy/Front Line University) part of your and your colleagues' Project Culture? (If yes ... are you sure? *V-e-r-y* sure?)

41.

After all, you *are* ... C.E.O. of Me Inc.... a thoroughly modern "virtual organization." Building—growing, nurturing—your Web of Contacts is a top priority. Age 23. Age 53. Create rituals: E.g., go through your Rolodex ... **every other week** ...and call a couple of folks you're out of touch with. **Religiously reserve every other Wednesday, say, to take someone in the Rolodex to lunch.** ("Rolodex Wednesday"?) Develop an eye for Talent, for a job well done, for WOW incarnate. Seek out those responsible. Add them to your virtual (or real) team.

The Nub

Build!

Build!

Build!

Build!

That's a no-brainer for Nike.

The Gap.

AOL.

Charles Schwab.

So … too … Me … and You. (I hope.)

And: Virtually All "Building" = Network Building = Talent Scouting.

One terrific project at McKinsey & Co. changed my life. (For sure.) And theirs. (It turned out.) It was a pushy project that disturbed the status quo. The Establishment was reluctant to sign on. (Understatement.) And so I scouted out and recruited non-Establishment types. Hot bods. *(Talent.)* Who were inflamed by the same cause that inflamed me.

We went our own way. And performed according to our own rhythms and metrics. One of the "rookies," Rajat Gupta, became Managing Director of the Whole Bloody Firm in 1994, 17 years after my "little" project started, 16 years after he "signed on," and 13 years after I left. (I got the boot!)

I repeat (loudly): "Talent Scouting" is not just for the Grand Old Men. I—at McKinsey—was in a Talent Scouting Mode as a … raw youth. In general, the idea of Building a Network of Kool Kindred Renegade Spirits need not be a task for the Elderly!

(Witness the American Revolution ... or damn near any Political or Scientific Revolution, for that matter. The Chief Renegades are rarely over ... **30.**)

T.T.D./Huntin' for Cool Dudes/Dudettes

1. **Always** (b-i-g word) be on the lookout for Talent. (Capital "T.") Cool Dudes/Dudettes to Hang With ... Conspire With ... Learn From. Any time you come across any interesting Dudes/Dudettes ... recruit them. (Think Che Guevara.)

2. AGE IS IRRELEVANT. This is a strategy for "powerless" 24-year-olds at least as much as for 44-year-olds. Mantra: **RECRUITING MISFITS—PIRATES IS ME.** (Daily. No baloney.)

3. Put this "On the Calendar." Little—*nothing?*—is more important. Is it "opportunism"? Sure! But it's also the product of a Plan ... or at least Constantly Attuned Awareness ... about Lurking Cool Dudes/Dudettes ... with whom I can make Wonderful/WOW Music.

4. **Collect ahead of need.** This idea goes much farther than filling a hole in the current project structure. The idea: You are always on the lookout for Talent. Find it. Sign it. That is, "sign up" the New Cool Dude to work on some little thing, any little thing. Now. Put her/him "in the loop" for all your communications and get-togethers of the (formal or informal) Cool Dude/Dudette Club. The Instinctive Talent Scouting Habit is all about opportunism and unanticipated needs.

42.

The Nub

Herman Miller's legendary chief Max DePree says a Great Organization ought to exhibit these traits:

* Truth

* Access

* Discipline

* Accountability

* Nourishment of persons

* Authenticity

* Justice

* Respect

* Hope

* Workable unity

* Tolerance

Sure it's good for GE, but I contend it holds, or could hold, for every Brand You/Me Inc. Again: You are CEO of

Me Inc. Your virtual org can aim to be as terrific as a ...
Herman Miller.(WHY NOT?)

I take Me Inc./Brand You seriously. I hope
you do."It" is an unparalleled ... opportunity ... to express
who you are/I am ... as a Human Being.

Brand You/Me Inc. is a "Corp." It deals with Clients.
Vendors. And other publics. It has "character," for good or
for ill. In my view—and yours?—it has Corporate Culture
as much as Intel or Charles Schwab. That is, it "stands
for"... *s-o-m-e-t-h-i-n-g.*

So why not—à la Max DePree above—make
that something ... **S**omething **G**reat?

T.T.D./Seriously Cool Characteristics
... of Me Inc.

1. Does Me Inc./Brand You have a Mission Statement?
If not ... Why Not? **(???!!!)** Begin to rough one out ...
now. Don't rush it. Give it a lot of thought. But do get
started ... NOW.

2. At Brand You/Me Inc.... what do you aspire to? Specifically? Again: Don't be hasty. Don't be glib. It is your life
... remember.

3. *As usual ... perform this exercise with kindred spirits.
It's personal, but it's also about ... a Community of Pals who
... Share the Same Important Values.*

43.

I once wrote a column on my personal "Hall of Fame," a dozen people I knew well and whom I admired greatly. (Most weren't "famous"...except perhaps to me.) My list of characteristics:

* *Self-invented.*

* *Ever-changing*...not bound by self-consistency.

* *Battered and bruised*...to play life's game vigorously is to necessarily accumulate scars, and even a gash or two.

* *Inquisitive*...to a fault.

* *Childlike, naïve* ... with an appetite for exploration that mimics a four-year-old's.

* *Free from the past.*

* *Comfortable* ... with the idea of life as a moving target.

* *Jolly*...they all laugh...a lot.

* *Audacious*...even a Bit Nuts.

* *Iconoclastic*...only happy, more or less, when they're on the Wrong Side of Conventional Wisdom.

* *Multidimensional* ... with flaws as great as their Virtues.

* *Honest* ... and Confused ... as all Truly Honest people are.

* *Larger than life* ... though often engaged in small ventures, they all paint their canvases in bold, colorful brush strokes; they embrace the Circus of Life ... rather than shrink from it.

These Make-a-Damn-Difference Attributes are as applicable to the 21-year-old as to the 51-year-old.

The Nub

Brand Yous ... take charge of their own lives. (The Anti-Dilbert Gang**!!!**) They are not water-walkers. They are ... in the best sense ... self-possessed. They know that Big Co. ain't going to take care of them from cradle (age 21) to grave (age 65). They know that they are ...

* Skills dependent

* Distinction dependent

* Network/Rolodex dependent

* Project (WOW Project) dependent

* Growth dependent

Brand Yous—age 21 as well as 51— are Leaders. Even if no one "reports to" them. (Officially.) (P.S.: No leader of a Revolution—ever—had anyone "officially" report to him. THINK ABOUT IT.) That is, through their independence, insouciance, and craft orientation, they "Model the Way," as my colleague (and leadership guru) Jim Kouzes puts it.

In short, regardless of circumstances ... big or small project ... impressive or unimpressive job titles ... **Brand Yous Lead** ... set the pace ... exude contagious enthusiasm.

T.T.D./Leaders All!

1. Brand You = **Leadership.** Right? If so, what does that mean ... precisely ... to you? Relative to your current project? Your next meeting (45 minutes from now)?

2. Consider the attributes of my personal Hall of Famers. Evaluate yourself on those—or like—dimensions. Get together with some close colleagues and talk about each item. Are these plausible aspirations? Pick one or two items off the list. Concoct specific steps—*relative to your current project*—to encompass these traits.

3. Become a student of leadership. What leaders do you admire? Why? (Be **very** specific. List **25** leadership traits—large and, particularly, small.) How can you emulate—in small ways, every day—some of those traits? (Again ... be specific. Very. And practical. Very.)

4. Forget your "job title." And your "official" project role. And ... your age. Leadership is **95** percent state of

mind. Will. Determination. Energy. Enthusiasm. Compassion. Hence: Perform a "state of mind" check before work ... at midday ... at 4 p.m. "Manage" (be in touch with) the Enthusiasm Vibes you give off. Or don't. This *is* practical stuff. If you focus on it you can make, with practice, a big difference in your self-presentation. (Talk, perhaps, to a sports psychologist about this.)

44.

The Nub

1. Power.

2. Nasty word.

3. Not.

4. Brand You "Freaks" = Accomplishment "Freaks."

5. Therefore: Power = Good.

6. Therefore: Effective Brand Yous = Power Freaks.

Let's get down off our Bloody High Horses about … P-O-W-E-R. Evil. Stalinist. Yes! Maoist. Yes! Hitleresque. Yes!

But on the other hand … Churchillian … and Rooseveltian … and Gandhian … and M. L. King-ian. Power Nuts. All.

That is … Determined to Get Things Done. Which happens o-n-l-y when you … Change Other People's Views about What's Possible. Russian serfs. (Lenin.) African Americans. (M. L. King, Jr.)

1. Brand Yous = Wanna Make a Difference.

2. Brand Yous = Acknowledge "Power."

3. Brand Yous = Use Power as a means to an end.

You need not be an egomaniac. Mostly. But successful "change agents" *do* have an inflated point of view of what's possible. (If they were "sensible," they'd never get out of bed in the morning to face the long odds against them. I.e., the possibility, 20 years ago, of Geeky Billy Gates trumping Almighty IBM.)

But they—mostly—keep it to themselves, if they're wise. You need not be an autocrat. Mostly. (Successful "change agents" *are* pretty obnoxious about The Basic Vision.)

The will and power to change minds ... is a Pretty Strong-Minded Thing. I.e.: YOU GOTTA BELIEVE ... Pretty Insanely ... in the Worth of Your Quest.

All I want to do here is ... to urge/convince you that "power" is not a "dirty" term. It is a term that all achievers accede to ... even if reluctantly.

T.T.D./Power Players!

1. Face it. Squarely. Though you are a "nice guy/gal" ... as Nouveau Brand You, you have A Point of View ... a Mission (your WOW Project) ... and you are therefore ... In the Business of Changing Minds.

Thence ... Power ... is your necessary Currency. Okay?

2. So ... **study** ... "politics." **Study** "Community Organizing." (E.g., Saul Alinsky's *Rules for Radicals* and

Reveille for Radicals.) **Study** the process of influencing others. (Start with Bob Cialdini's brilliant book *Influence*.)

3. Don't be a jerk! Or, rather: **Don't pretend you are "above politics."** Or … "not into power." No one who accomplishes anything worthy of note is "above politics" or oblivious to the ebb and flow of power.

4. Think systematically about your base of power. From what does it derive? (Towering competence at something? Exceptional oratorical flair? World-class schmoozing-networking skills? Brilliance at talent-spotting? An abnormal dose of empathy?) How (specifically) do/can you change minds?

(5. We'll have lots more to say about this in our forthcoming *the Power + Implementation50*. An indication of our view of power: it merits an entire book in this *Reinventing Work 50List* series!)

45.

Folks must brag about Your Work/Projects … if you're to succeed as Brand You. Forget if-you-build-it-they-will-come! Of course … Good Work Comes First. But you also need to publicize it, gather Testimonials, and consciously build B-U-Z-Z.

The Nub

Brand You = Marketing Prowess.

No, you don't have to be as Good as Martha Stewart or Michael Jordan. But you must not dismiss "marketing" as something for the "crass commercial folks who sell M&Ms."

1. "Marketing" = "Aura" (around Tom Peters or Joan Doaks)

2. Marketing = "Known For"

3. Marketing = Image

4. Marketing = People Talking/Buzzing About You

The Big Idea here: For you—and me!—as for Pepsi, "IF YOU BUILD IT THEY WILL COME" … IS A BANKRUPT MARKETING STRATEGY.

MARKETING =
PROACTIVE =
UN-ACCIDENTAL BUZZ-BUILDING.

Period.

T.T.D./ Proactive "Marketing"

1. **So what have you done ... T-O-D-A-Y ... to "advertise" Y-o-u? To let the World (locally, at least) know that you are ... Alive ... Well ... Cool ... and Uniquely Contributing?**

2. Become a Serious Student of Marketing/Word-of-Mouth Marketing. Become conversant with the ideas, the terminology. Message: Don't shy away from "marketing lingo" as it applies to ... y-o-u. Take a course (or two ... or five) in marketing. Learn marketing skills. Know your markets ... and the bases of your marketability.

3. Bottom Line: **Construct a Formal Word-of-Mouth Marketing Plan.** Key Word: F-O-R-M-A-L. To bump yourself into high gear, read and absorb Regis McKenna's classic *Relationship Marketing*.

45a.

No "real" product... and the World's Greatest Marketing Plan won't do you an iota's worth of good.

The Nub

William Bridges recounts this profound exchange, slightly abridged, in his book *Creating You & Co.*:

Bridges: "What is your product?"
Client: "You mean the company's product?"

B: "No, I mean yours."
C: "Well, I'm in Personnel."

B: "Great. Good field. What's your product?"
C: "I am a compensation-and-benefits specialist."

B: "Interesting role. But what's your *product*?"
C: "Compensation-and-benefits?"

B: "That's not really a product. A product is something that somebody buys.... It confers an advantage, it meets a need. Comp-and-benefits systems are just organizational furniture."

In the postjob world employees need to forget their jobs and start looking for the work that needs doing. ... Your market isn't "the job market." [It] is the people around you who have unmet needs. ... You aren't looking for "jobs," but rather "opportunities." ...

You should stop thinking like an employee and start thinking like an opportunity-minded vendor. ... Every employee is in direct competition with external vendors ... happy to bring the vendor's mindset to any task currently being done by an employee....

Change is the enemy of people ... trying to hold on to their jobs ... [and] the friend of people who take this marketing approach.... This means that career planning needs to be a process very similar to ... strategic business planning within a small start-up company.

* * *

You/Me/Brand Us = Product/Marketing

* * *

Brand You, essence of:

What "Service" do you/I sell ... that is Worth Paying For? If we do "Sell" something "Worth Paying For" ... how do We "market" it?

Tom Peters on Tom Peters:

I think my work has "merit."
I think it is "academically grounded."

But I am ... t-o-t-a-l-l-y aware ... that if no one will pay me to show up, well ... then:

My Impact = Zero.
No customers ... No Impact. Period.

Which means ... I've got to have an ... identifiable "product." RIGHT?

So:

THINK P-R-O-D-U-C-T.
WHAT PRODUCT DO YOU OFFER THAT IS CLEARLY ... WORTH P-A-Y-I-N-G GOOD MONEY FOR?

If you are offended by the above ... you are, I fear ... Roadkill on the White Collar Highway.

T.T.D./ P-r-o-d-u-c-t

1. T-h-i-n-k p-r-o-d-u-c-t. Review the Bridges exchange above. Define your "product." Carefully.

Now. Succinctly. Convincingly. Test your definition out on others ... of all stripes. (Including the plumber and the grocer and the cabbie and the architect who lives next door.)

2. More Bridges. Consider his exact terms:

WORK THAT NEEDS DOING ... UNMET NEEDS ... OPPORTUNITY-MINDED VENDOR ... VENDOR'S MINDSET ... CAREER PLANNING = STRATEGIC BUSINESS PLANNING.

I **l-o-v-e** all this**!** Think about it. Define it (these terms) in ways that relate personally/compellingly to you. (Please stick to Bridges's exact terminology.)

3. **What is d-i-f-f-e-r-e-n-t about m-y p-r-o-d-u-c-t?** Fair question, eh? Gillette must provide an unequivocal answer. **Why not you?**

46.

Brand You: The Whole World really is Your Oyster. (If you've got a **SERIOUSLY COOL PRODUCT** to sell... *and* a "brand structure" to support it... *and* Imagination ... *and* Determination ... *and* the Web.)

The Nub

It *is* a new game. If your—my!—"stuff" is Cool, we can become "Global" ... overnight ... or at least, pretty darn quickly.

I'm not suggesting it's an imperative. I'm simply saying that **The Force Is With You** ... courtesy of, among other (big) things ... the Web.

If you've got something terribly cool/proprietary/rockin' to say ... say it ...**to the World.**

DON'T HESITATE.

T.T.D./ Brand You as Global Force!

1. I am not hammering on this. But I am raising it gently ... as something to keep in mind. I am arguing that if you "Do Breathtakingly Cool Stuff" ... the World may well be Your Oyster ... far sooner than you think ... age 18 ... or 88. So: Is your "Stuff" Cool? Seriously Cool?

G-l-o-b-a-l Cool?

(P.S.: You won't know until you try.)

2. "Global" is 96+ percent a frame of mind. (Really.) If you feel good about "your stuff" ... don't be shy. Hawk it to ... T-h-e W-o-r-l-d. **(Really.)** I.e.: Start a Purposefully Global Web Conversation ... at your site. **Now.**

47.

Everyone lives by selling something.
—Robert Louis Stevenson

What I am doing is selling myself. Intellectually I think I understand that, but emotionally I didn't until I experienced the pain of constantly putting myself on the line and facing rejection. It makes sense to look at yourself as a work in progress and to define your core assets and then sell them to the marketplace. The question ultimately is, "Are you willing to do what it takes to get the opportunity you want?"

—Susan Gould et al., in *Free Agents*, quoting an executive making a career transition

The Nub

Sales is not a dirty word for "us professionals." If you want to get on a certain project team ...

"Sell-the-Hell-Out-of-Yourself."

It's gospel truth for accountants at Arthur Andersen ... and for software programmers at Oracle ... and, of course, for Martha Stewart.

Sell.

Sell.

Sell.

Sell.

Sell.

Sell.

Sell.

If you are appalled or distressed by the word ("sell"), well … Worry … a lot. I.e.: Circa 2000 … Get a Life. (Sorry for the harshness. 'Tis the hour for Honesty.)

Sure, I know a lot of fine/gifted/WOW-ing folks aren't great at sales … makes them uncomfortable as all get out. They hate the idea of "pushing" themselves. They're shy, reticent, just want to concentrate on the work. All I can say is: **Ya gotta do it. (Sales, that is.)** You don't have to be "great" at it. It doesn't have to be your main focus, but you cannot ignore it. So accept you've got to do it … put in the time … and do it succinctly and well.

T.T.D./ Sell, Baby, Sell!

1. **Create a Clean/Clear/Crisp/Compelling "Selling Proposition."** (It's as important for Mary Jones, accountant, as for Calvin Klein.)

2. Do you "obsess"—right word!—on "Sales"? Please … take this s-e-r-i-o-u-s-l-y. The Best "senior partners" at the Big Professional Service Firms are as "Sales Oriented" as Da Guy who sells Used Cars. (Again: No baloney.) (See also our *the Professional Service Firm50*.)

48.

That means telling the prospective Client what the Real Price will be for a three-month project. (And it had better be aggressive, so you can pay for the significant research required to do a WOW job.) It means gathering the nerve to ask the Chairwoman for her support. "Closing" is a learned skill. (So … learn it.)

The Nub

Closers.

Bless them.

Brand You = Me Inc.

Brand You = Product. (Clear. Distinct.)

Brand You = Convey the Benefits of the Product.

Brand You = Close! (The Sale.)

No, you don't need to be a … Sales Houdini. But you do need to stop denigrating Sales … and the Sales Process.

I am a … w-i-m-p.

But life has taught me … in the last 15+ years … to Ask for the Sale. Life (Brand You) = Necessity.

It's Damn Hard. Excruciatingly Hard Work. (For me, anyway.) But: It must be done.

T.T.D./Close!

1. You are Brand You. **You are Worth It.** So… Ask for the Business.

49.

The Nub

It was 2:28 a.m., June 20, 1999. I woke up with a start. I was in my hotel room in Washington, by myself. I had spent the day—well, most of it—reading *Paul Rand,* by Steven Heller. Rand was one of this century's great designers/graphic artists; his design-identity miracles were performed for everyone from *Esquire* magazine to IBM to UPS.

But what struck me was Rand's life pattern. He became convinced that he had something to offer. And he was a sponge for new ideas … from around the world. (An American globalist … 60 years ago. Quite a deal.) So he became a job-hopper. He went from here to there. Without a thought for money. He was determined to follow/ shape his encompassing dream. One payroll for life, I'm sure from what I read, never crossed his mind. Networker par excellence? Amen! Mentors helped him at every step. But old-fashioned "logo loyalty"? Never.

Hence, it struck me (right words) that Rand was Quintessential Brand You. That the essence of Brand You is a Commitment to Growth … at almost any cost. A commitment to Free Expression and Personal Excellence...at almost any cost.

"Just Say 'No'" to Loyalty!

1. **ARE YOU COMMITTED TO EXCEL-LENCE? ARE YOU COMMITTED TO MAKING A DIFFERENCE? DO YOU UNDERSTAND THE SACRIFICES THAT ARE DEMANDED?** (I.e.: No job security. The need to be hyper-flexible... and go, on more or less a moment's notice, to the Home of the Next Cool-Growth Opportunity.)

IF YOU DON'T GET THIS ... YOU WILL STRUGGLE WITH THE BRAND YOU IDEA.

(Sorry.) (Welcome to the New Millennium.)

50.

The Nub

* New Economy.

* Unit-of-One.

* Independence.

* Freedom.

* Liberation.

* Self-reliance.

* Icon-woman.

* C-o-o-l Dude/Dudette.

* Cool Shit.

* WOW!Projects.(Or Bust.)

* Imagination Inc.

* Restless Renegade.

MY WORK MATTERS.

(That's it.)

1. I AM ME INC.

SEE ME/HEAR ME R-O-A-R.

I MATTER.

MY WORK MATTERS.

(It sounds corny, even embarrassing, but do it: Repeat the above while looking in a mirror.)

2. **Brand You Rules!** (*You* can do it!)

GOOD LUCK!

(THIS IS COOL.)

The Movement!

How audacious! Start a Movement?! We plan to do just that.

Title: The Work Matters!

(Or: The Anti-Dilbert Movement.)

We are sick and tired of whining about lousy bosses. (Or companies.) It is—as we see it—our life. To live … or lose. To form … or allow to be formed.

Dilbert is hilarious. (I.e., on the money.) And there's the rub. Dilbert stands not only for cynicism (an emotion I appreciate) but also for the de facto acceptance of power-less-ness. Power-less-ness … at the coolest time in centuries to make a mark. And that is where I draw the line!

It is my life. To live fully. Or not. And I damn well intend to live it fully. And I don't think I'm alone.

So my colleagues and I are … audaciously … starting

The Work Matters!

Movement. And we invite you to join us. Cost of membership: the time it takes to type www.tompeters.com into your computer.

Welcome aboard!

(P.S.: You may have noted the oversized  in the paragraphs above. No accident. That is our symbol … the exclamation mark … about as far from Dilbert as one can get, eh?)

www.tompeters.com

RECOMMENDED READING

CREATING YOU & CO: LEARN TO THINK LIKE THE CEO OF YOUR OWN CAREER, by William Bridges (Reading, MA: Addison-Wesley, 1997). A superb piece of work!

RUNNING A ONE-PERSON BUSINESS, by Claude Whitmyer, Salli Rasberry, and Michael Phillips (Berkeley: Ten Speed Press, 1989). A practical primer ... with soul!

WE ARE ALL SELF-EMPLOYED, by Cliff Hakim (Berrett-Koehler Publishers, 1994). A clearly worthwhile read.

INC. YOUR DREAMS, by Rebecca Maddox (New York: Viking, 1995). Maddox writes brilliantly for "any woman who is thinking about her own business." But it is really for all of us.

THE CAREER IS DEAD: LONG LIVE THE CAREER, by Douglas Hall et al. (San Francisco: Jossey-Bass, 1996). An academic ... but very readable ... approach to the new world of work.

TAKING RESPONSIBILITY: SELF-RELIANCE AND THE ACCOUNTABLE LIFE, by Nathaniel Branden (New York: Simon & Schuster, 1996). The modern-day Emerson waxes eloquent. I LOVE THIS BOOK.

THE 7 HABITS OF HIGHLY EFFECTIVE PEOPLE, by Stephen Covey (New York: Simon & Schuster, 1989). Great guide for Brand Yous!

MASTERY, by George Leonard (New York: Dutton, 1991). The title says it all...a beautiful book.

THE MAKING OF A CHEF, by Michael Ruhlman (New York: Henry Holt, 1997). A marvelous inside look at the Pursuit of Mastery and the Making of Brand You.

LIFE WORK, by Donald Hall (Boston: Beacon Press, 1993). Poet-essayist Hall talks movingly about Work that Matters.

LIVING YOUR LIFE OUT LOUD, by Salli Rasberry and Padi Selwyn (New York: Minstrel Books, 1995). Extremely thoughtful...starting with that great title!

WHAT THEY DON'T TEACH YOU AT HARVARD BUSINESS SCHOOL, by Mark McCormack (New York: Bantam, 1984). No. 1 sports agent McCormack provides a boatload of wisdom and practical advice.

EMOTIONAL INTELLIGENCE, by Daniel Goleman (New York: Bantam, 1995). Brand You must master human relationships!

DIFFICULT CONVERSATIONS: HOW TO DISCUSS WHAT MATTERS MOST, by Douglas Stone, Bruce Patton, and Sheila Heen (New York: Viking, 1999). A brilliant book—the best I've ever read—on the art of communicating one-on-one...a Brand You imperative.

THE FOUNTAINHEAD, by Ayn Rand (New York: New American Library, 1943). Talk about a radical Brand You proponent!

ACKNOWLEDGMENTS

Alan Webber, *Fast Company* co-creator ... who encouraged me to focus on this topic, and then worked with me on its first, big public exposure in his magazine. Erik Hansen ... project manager for this book and chief architect, along with Julie Anixter and Ken Silvia, of **The Movement!** (I.e.: The Work Matters!) Sonny Mehta ... who instantly saw the possibilities for this unique series of books. Sebastian Stuart and Edward Kastenmeier ... for thoughtful and meticulous editing.

Esther Newberg at ICM ... who worked to create this unusual book project/series with her usual flair and tenacity. Knopf Design Guru Chip Kidd ... who invented the look and feel of this series. Pat Johnson ... vigorous believer and Knopf marketing maestro. Patrik Jonsson and Jim Napolitano at Mulberry Studio ... for translating my original hen scratchings—yes, all of my first drafts are Bic on Yellow Pad—into a usable ms. Sue Bencuya ... for fact-checking. Elyse Friedman, Martha Lawler, and Vincent Renstrom ... for their editorial expertise. Katherine Hourigan, without whose assistance none of this would actually have happened ... Mel Rosenthal, who helped eliminate errors and inconsistencies ... Andy Hughes and Quinn O'Neill, who turned these words into the bound book you now hold in your hands ... Merri Ann Morrell, whose herculean efforts helped make these books possible. Ian Thomson and Michelle Rotzin ... for minding the store at The Tom Peters Company/Palo Alto.

Martha, Oprah, MJ et al.... who demonstrate the possibility of Brand You every day. (Have you noticed that true Brand Yous don't need full names?)

And: Susan Sargent ... who inspires me by example every frenzied day!

Tom Peters
West Tinmouth, Vermont
4 August 1999

Tom Peters is the co-author of *In Search of Excellence* (with Robert H. Waterman, Jr.) and *A Passion for Excellence* (with Nancy Austin), and the author of *Thriving on Chaos*, *Liberation Management*, *The Tom Peters Seminar*, *The Pursuit of Wow!*, *The Circle of Innovation*, and the *Reinventing Work* series. He is the founder of the Tom Peters Company, with offices in Palo Alto, Boston, Chicago, Cincinnati, and London. He and his family live on a farm in Vermont and an island off the Massachusetts coast, thanks to the information technology revolution. He can be reached at **tom@tompeters.com.**

tompeters.com

And now it's easy to get WOW!ed
with Tom anywhere:

<u>See</u> Tom Peters at a live one-day
seminar near you!
www.lessonsinleadership.com
1-800-873-3451

<u>Bring WOW! Projects to your
desktop computer</u>!
www.ninthhouse.com
1-800-304-4951

<u>See</u> Tom on Yahoo! Broadcast
Services this fall!
www.leadership.broadcast.com

<u>Schedule</u> Tom to talk to your group!
michellerotzin@tompeters.com

<u>Learn about Training and
Consulting</u> for your business!
www.tompeters.com
1-888-221-8685